ODES FOR VICTORIOUS ATHLETES

Johns Hopkins
New Translations
from Antiquity

Pindar

ODES FOR VICTORIOUS ATHLETES

Translated with an introduction
by Anne Pippin Burnett

The Johns Hopkins University Press
Baltimore

The Johns Hopkins University Press
2715 North Charles Street
Baltimore, Maryland 21218-4363
www.press.jhu.edu

These translations are based on the text of Bruno Snell and Herwig Maehler, *Pindari Carmina*, pt. 1 (Leipzig: Teubner, 1987).

Library of Congress Cataloging-in-Publication Data

Pindar.
  [Works. English. 2010]
  Odes for victorious athletes / Pindar ; translated with an introduction
  by Anne Pippin Burnett.
      p. cm. — (Johns Hopkins New Translations from Antiquity)
  Includes bibliographical references.
  ISBN-13: 978-0-8018-9574-6 (hardcover : alk. paper)
  ISBN-10: 0-8018-9574-X (hardcover : alk. paper)
  ISBN-13: 978-0-8018-9575-3 (pbk. : alk. paper)
  ISBN-10: 0-8018-9575-8 (pbk. : alk. paper)
  1. Pindar—Translations into English. 2. Laudatory poetry, Greek—Translations into
English. 3. Athletics—Greece—Poetry. 4. Games—Greece—Poetry. I. Burnett, Anne
Pippin, 1925– II. Title.
PA4275.E5B87 2010
884'.01—dc22   2009048736

A catalog record for this book is available from the British Library.

Special discounts are available for bulk purchases of this book. For more information, please contact Special Sales at 410-516-6936 or specialsales@press.jhu.edu.

for Wendy and David

Contents

Introduction

Pindar's songs for victorious Greek athletes often surprise the modern ear with the complexity of their magnificence but also with their lack of immediate involvement. We know that these works were proudly commissioned and sung before audiences made up of present, past, and future contenders, but on first acquaintance it is hard to understand the songs' success with such listeners. They list places and prizes, and they sometimes employ figures of speech derived from the cast of a discus or the course of a lance, but athletic matters are not their immediate concern. Their words do not revive a particular winning ploy, the moment of the opponent's fall, or the saving swerve of a clever charioteer. Even the victor's chosen event may be left obscure—was he a runner, or perhaps a boxer? Instead, though they were commissioned to honor boys and men distinguished for muscle and skill, Pindar's victory odes entertain their listeners with local nymphs and heroes, with bits of legend and myth, and with self-regarding discussions of their own purpose and style. To enjoy them, a present-day reader needs only a slight knowledge of ancient sport but a somewhat fuller sense of the society that chose this mode for celebrating its champions.

In the Greece of Pindar's time (the first half of the fifth century BC), foot soldiers had replaced cavalry as the decisive force in battle, and in consequence, the power of the old landed families was diminishing. As horse-rearing aristocrats, these men had traditionally been responsible for the survival of all who lived around them, dealing with common friends and enemies, but their alliances and actions no longer determined a city's external policies. Nor did men of this class continue to be the only effective representatives of the community as it arranged for protective support from gods and daimonic powers, for temples could now be built and elaborate civic rituals organized by commercial wealth. Nevertheless, one spectacular approach to divine favor was still controlled by the nobility, for at the festivals where formal strife was dedicated to heroes or gods, they alone were prepared to make the expenditure of force and daring that was required if the immortals were to be pleased.

The Hellenic contender in an athletic competition offered his inher-

1

ited strength, his acquired training, and his own concentrated courage, as well as his blood, his bones, and possibly his life, for the delight of supernatural spectators who might in return bestow favor upon the athlete, his family, and his community. Lesser contests honored local deities everywhere, but there were four great festivals—two dedicted to Zeus (at Olympia and at Nemea), one honoring Apollo (at Delphi), and one for Poseidon (at the Isthmos, near Corinth). In any given year, at least one of these would be held, always with much the same schedule of events, as the athlete, boy or man, either faced a field of like competitors (in running, jumping, casting spear or discus, riding a horse, driving a mule-cart or chariot) or met a single opponent (in wrestling, boxing, or the rough mixture of these called the *pankration*). The so-called pentathlon, a late development (Isthmian 1.26), included trials of both sorts.

At the games athletes put themselves and their kin on trial as a gift to a deity—Zeus, Apollo, or Poseidon—and that power signalled his pleasure by touching a winner with the magic of success. Divine contact would in an instant give decisive control to one contestant, and this return gift was then reified in a crown (of olive, bay, dried parsley, or celery leaves) that was placed on the victor's head in the final prize-giving ceremonies. Such a crown was proof of a special relationship between the victor and the god from whose festival it came, one that would endure and would include as well the athlete's family and those who lived near him. All this was made clear when at the close of a particular contest the herald announced not just the name of the victor but also those of his father and of his city. That voice, sounding in the sacred precinct, fixed an indestructible prestige (*kudos*) upon victor, house, and community, but if this endowment was to be reflected in their worldly condition, it needed to be transformed into the fame (*kleos*) that lived on men's tongues. Only the gods could ensure an ultimate remembrance of mortal achievements, but they could be influenced by hymns and petitions, and meanwhile, men, by combining names and deeds with music and motion, could confer a kind of permanence:

> Noble deeds we can mirror only when
> garlanded Memory joins us in chanted
> fame-bearing song, due ransom for toil (Nemean 7.14–6)

One who took a crown at the great games, whether boy or man, was that night joined by his friends in a wild fire-lit revel that took place on the spot (at Olympia, "the whole sacred glade feasted and sang," Olympian 10, 76–7). When, weeks or months later, he and his party brought the prize back to his city, the athlete's household staged a formal celebration through which the victor shared his success with his community. Friends, neighbors, and relatives (all male) would be invited to a victory banquet, but this was no ordinary symposium with entertainment by acrobats and flute-girls. Instead, when the tables had been removed but wine still circulated freely, a group of free-born boys or young men—the best and handsomest of local singers—would burst in with a version of the rowdy victory-night revel. The singers represented the athlete's companions, but, though they brought something of the victory night into the banquet, they also spoke for the entire community as a public chorus might when engaged in a cult celebration. These two strains, one of spontaneous disorder, the other of formal convention, are reflected throughout Pindar's epinician songs in language that can be at one moment familiar, proverbial, even teasing, at the next solemn and consciously elegant.

A citizen of Thebes, Pindar, was—in his own time and ever since—the most famous of the poets who designed victory performances. Sometimes he travelled to the victor's city, sometimes he sent a messenger, but however they were conveyed his odes were produced in spaces private or public, simple or palatial, in locations as far apart as Tenedos in the east, Akragas in the west, Thrace in the north, and Cyrene in the south. Some odes were short, some long, and while some were addressed to beardless boys, others hailed experienced athletes or offered their commissioned praise to rulers who gave the reins of their horses into the hands of professionals. Yet in spite of this disparity, all of his victory songs show certain regular features. To begin with, all are strongly traditional, their melodies taken from a common stock known to all men of education, with answering choreography defined by the particular performance space. The performers sang in unison as they danced—six, eight, or twelve of them, unless this was a palace—sometimes murmuring, sometimes shouting as they "stepped light" (Olympian 14.17) to the sounds of a lyre or the "breath of Aiolian pipes" (Nemean 3.79).

The words that Pindar provided for such performances emphasize the solemn formality of these festive occasions, for they were marked by the vowel sounds that characterized most songs meant for a plurality of voices (the so-called Doric dialect). The length of each Greek syllable was fixed—to some a dancer could take just one step, to others he might take two, or pause for an instant—and short patterned phrases were gathered into larger rhythmic units, which would be repeated once or many times, as the sense of the song evolved. As a rule the sequence of such stanzas took a triadic form, as exactly responding pairs called *strophe* and *antistrophe* were marked off by a third stanza of slightly different form called an *epode*. There might be only one such triad (as in Olympian 12) or there might be several (Pythian 4 has thirteen), but since repeating rhythms indicate movements and musical phrases that likewise repeat, an ode of any length was evidently filled with its own echoes, both of sound and of gesture. As one group of dancers put it, "the voice of loud celebration" was made to wear the "Dorian sandal" of traditional choral modes (Olympian 3.4–6).

Paradoxically enough, another convention that Pindar embraced with evident pleasure was that of a pretended spontaneity. The victor's community knew that a troupe of young men were rehearsing the work of a famous poet, but in performance the dancers presented themselves as spurred by the moment. Speaking as one or as many, they repeatedly described themselves as a *komos,* a disorderly drunken group that bursts into the house of a friend. Sometimes they pretended to come straight from the victor's triumph ("I come with a musical message!" Pythian 2.3), or to be still collecting themselves at his gate (Isthmian 8.1–5), and they repeatedly insisted on the impromptu nature of their performance. In this character they may give themselves encouragement ("Wild shouts suit Aristokleidas!" Nemean 3.67) or boast of their skills ("I know a short-cut!" Pythian 4.247–8); they might scold themselves ("but, o my mouth, spit out this tale," Olympian 9.35–6) and seem to engage their listeners directly ("Friends, did I stray from the plain path I followed before?" Pythian 11.37–8). Yet even as with well-rehearsed phrases they claimed to be acting on impulse, Pindar's performers would also describe their work as orderly and measured ("My given task is to garland this man with Aeolic song cast in equestrian mode," Olympian 1.101), sometimes speaking for the professional poet who had created their songs ("since my voice has been hired for a wage," Pythian 11.40, cf. Isthmian 2.6–11). Theirs was a polished performance derived from a rough original, and this double fact was plainly stated at the opening of Olympian 9 (lines 1–5):

> The Archilochos chant—
> "Victor triumphant!"
>   shouted three times—could

open the revel when Epharmostos
danced with his friends close by the
Kronian hill, but today a volley of   at Olympia
   far-flying shafts like these must
   sweep from the bows of the Muses . . .

While they pretend to be improvisations, Pindar's odes show a set of common characteristics that reflect the essential nature of the great games. The victory that the singers honor was an offering made to a god, and all of these songs are sanctifiecd through their use of the sonorous Doric dialect that flavoured certain cult chants. The dancers, moreover, like sacred celebrants, often marked their own actions with ritualizing self-commentary, like the Aiginetan boys who chant, "I stop my light feet and take breath," as they do exactly that (Nemean 8.19). And in almost every song, the singers call upon otherworldly powers—Graces, Muses, local nymphs, heroes or heroines, or Panhellenic gods, most often Zeus—with prayers and invocations. Communication with eternal forces is established early or late in each song, while the singers' voices pursue their central task of causing certain names and deeds to resound through time —brothers, uncles, fathers, grandfathers are announced along with the victor, as are lists of contests attended and prizes taken (golden cups, tripods, or woolly cloaks), all given permanence by effective gestures and musical phrases. Often totals are calculated—Olympian 13 counts more than sixty familial crowns, then concludes that it would be "easier to number the sands of the sea" (line 46).

Sung praise gave the athlete's success an enduring glory that illumined the entire community. Nevertheless, if this new status was to be immediately experienced by all, the celebrating guests needed access to the magical instant when victory was determined, and it was this ultimate requirement that let Pindar exercise his special talents to their fullest. For every major ode, he composed a passage, brief or extended, in which the *komos*, like a cultic chorus, recreated a mythic marvel so that the immediate festivity was invaded by a timeless event. The audience witnessed a moment in which a daimonic force entered the human scheme, but the singers did not narrate their episode like a bard, nor did they separate to take individual voices, like actors in the theater. Instead, a formal rhetorical figure, or perhaps a list of some sort, would suddenly produce a scene from a particular legend. There might sometimes be a rough summary of a tale, followed before long by a focussed presentation of a fragmentary episode, but these mythic sketches were usually without beginning, middle, or end. (The exception is at Pythian 4.70, where a beginning is explicitly sought, but all is exceptional in that enormous song.)

In Pindar's mythic passages, minimal allusions are brought together so as to produce an image sharp enough to mark the listener's immediate sensory experience, and then the story is abandoned. Sometimes the moment becomes actual by way of a visualized object, as with the golden bit that Athena leaves for Bellerophon (Olympian 13.65–72), or the elaborate cup that Telamon hands to Herakles at his wedding celebration (Isthmian 6.40). A like effect may be wrought by more complex means, as with the colored patches of light that play over the newborn Iamos, and the honeyed flavor of his "venomous" food (Olympian 6.55–6 and 47). Sometimes the sense of immediacy derives from creatures imbued with perceived vitality, like the three silvery snakes that attack the new-built walls of Troy (Olympian 8.37), the roaring lions that flee from Battos (Pythian 5.57–62), or the panting bestial corpses that a six-year old Achilles carries to Chiron (Nemean 3.46–9). At other times listeners may seem to hear a voice from another realm as singers pronounce the words of a divinity in action—those of Apollo as he strides through flames to rescue the unborn Asklepios (Pythian 3.40–2), those of Themis as she decides the outcome of strife between Zeus and Poseidon (Isthmian 8.38–49), or those of Zeus as he offers Pollux the power to revive his brother (Nemean 10.83–90). Each mythic reconstruction works its own momentary magic, then quickly dissolves, but hosts and guests have all felt a brief daimonic presence while at the same time the victor's achievement has been associated with an action that defies both space and time. The light of the victor's glory, reinforced by the light of the mythic moment, now rests upon all as a "god-given splendor" (Pythian 8.97).

In the course of an ode, Pindar's singers led a victor and his gathered friends into a state of common exaltation as they shared in an experience of direct divine favor. This revelation was the ultimate aim of the victory performance, but such bliss had its dangers, since all men also shared something of Tantalos's inability to digest too much happiness (Olympian 1.55–6), something of Ixion's tendency to overreach (Pythian 2.26–9). Extreme joy might lead to impious presumption, and this is why the victory songs were liberally sprinkled with pithy sayings about mortal limitations. Proverbs turn up at any point, with an air of relevance or of total

inconsequence, as they cap victory lists, introduce or cut off mythic recon-
structions, or simply interrupt. Again and again, the crowned athlete and
his celebrating friends are reminded that all men, whether they enjoy lei-
sure or are forced to work, are alike in facing death. They are told that "No
man is or ever will be without his due share of trouble" (Pythian 5.54), that
"the gods ever provide two evils with each single good" (Pythian 3.81–2),
and that "Rich and poor together move towards death's boundary" (Ne-
mean 7.19–20). Human success is always open to reversal from higher
powers, just as winds will always change (Olympian 7.94–5, Pythian
12.31–2), and victors like all others must remember that "the mortal limbs
that today are wrapped in splendor will in the end be clothed in earth"
(Nemean 11.15–6). Even a man who, victorious himself, sees his son
crowned at Delphi, "will never walk the bronze floors of heaven, though
among mortal joys he may visit the furthest ports" (Pythian 10.22–9).

With dancers, guests, and hosts gilded by the "undimmed radiance"
of victory (Isthmian 3/4.59–60) but at the same time made conscious of
their own mortality, the Pindaric ode could come to an end. It might close
with a prayer for further glories ("let him take garlands from Pytho and
Elis . . . !" Isthmian 1. 66), or with mention of some detail of the immedi-
ate ceremony (Olympian 9.111–2 places a crown on the altar of the local
hero). If it praised a boy, the song might end with recognition of his
trainer's skill. Nemean 4 ends by imagining an ode for Melesias. What-
ever their final syllables, however, the singers would finish by standing for
a moment in fulfilled silence. Then the entire company, their noble cour-
age reaffirmed, would enter the state of radiant joy that Pindar called
euphrosyna, "best healer after a trial" (Nemean 4.1, cf. Pythian 4.129,
10.40, 11.45, Isthmian 3/4.10), as the unrehearsed part of the celebration
began.

At the end of his own century, Pindar was lampooned by Aristophanes as
tedious and parasitic because he worked for pay (*Birds* 939), but he was
soon recognized as one of the greatest of Greek poets. His house in
Thebes was preserved into Roman times, and at Delphi visitors were
shown a throne in which he was said to have sat while singing hymns to
Apollo. Alexandrian scholars collected and edited what could be found of
his work, classifying individual pieces according to function, grouping the
victory hymns by festival, and adding commentary. In this form the odes
came into the hands of Horace and other Roman writers, who judged

them pompous but admirable and worthy of imitation. Forgotten in the Middle Ages, Pindar was rediscovered in the Renaissance, and in mid-sixteenth-century France, Ronsard, the "prince of poets," mimicked the "glorious fury" of his exclamations and digressions and boasted that he had "Pindarized." As time went on, this "divine Pindar" began to be criticized for being "led rather by the demon of poetry than by reason" (Boileau, "Discours sur l'Ode," 1693), but in the eighteenth century Goethe, Hölderlin, and Schiller continued to be enthusiastic, and Schlegel, at the conclusion of his "On the Study of Greek Poetry" spoke of Pindar's "intense sensibility, nobility of thought, magnificence of imagination, dignity of language, and authority of rhythm."* The reaction of Victorian England was mixed and Tennyson found in the odes "long tracts of gravel, with immensely large nuggets embedded."† Nevertheless, distinguished scholarly studies of Pindaric text, metrics, dialect, compositional conventions, mythic traditions, images, and favorite concepts have come continuously from Britain, the continent, and North America throughout the nineteenth and twentieth centuries. At the present moment the odes are studied principally for their reflections of the politics and society of early fifth-century Greece, but they are enduring examples of how poetry can impose a transforming experience upon its listener.

*F. Schlegel, *On the Study of Greek Poetry,* tr. S. Barnett (Albany: State University of New York Press, 2001), 94.
†Quoted by Halam Tennyson, *Alfred Lord Tennyson, a Memoir,* ii (New York: Macmillan, 1897), 499.

ODES FOR VICTORIOUS ATHLETES

For Hieron, ruler of Syracuse in Sicily, to celebrate the victory of his race-horse, Pherenikos. Since 478 BC, when he succeeded his brother Gelo, Hieron had been the richest and most powerful man in Sicily, the dominant partner in his alliance with Theron, the ruler of Akragas, and in full control of the eastern section of the island. With an Olympic crown, a man of such power had no match, which is why this song begins with a search for parallel superlatives; it is also why its mythic section contrasts a father who did not know how to receive a gift of immortality with a son who understood how to use divine favor.

To an audience who has been dining, the singers give a reformed version of a tale of divine cannibalism. The old story was that Tantalos, having been made immortal, had offered his son as a feast for visiting gods and that Demeter had taken a bite (lines 45–53), but the disappearance of Pelops is now given a more appetizing explanation (lines 40–44).

For other odes commissioned by Hieron, see Pythian 1, 2, and 3.
476 BC

1. Water is best, but gold, like a blazing fire in the night,
dominates all magnificent wealth and
if, o my heart, you would speak of
athletic trials
look for no star in the day's empty air that   5
shines with more warmth than the sun—no other
    games shall we hail as
greater than those at Olympia,
source of the many-voiced
hymn that embraces the thoughts of
singers who gather to celebrate Zeus at   10
Hieron's rich and fortunate hearth!

His lawful scepter he wields in cattle-rich Sicily where,
reaping the best of all that is fine,

he knows an increase of splendor in
song at its best,   15
such as we make at his table, like children at
play. So take down the Dorian
   lyre from its peg if your
mind was enslaved to sweet thoughts by the
glory of Pisa, or
by Pherenikos when, unwhipped, he   20
ran beside Alpheos, lending himself to the course
while to his horse-loving lord, ruler of

ep. Syracuse, he brought triumph as mate! His
   glory now shines in the
populous city of Lydian Pelops, he who
roused the desire of Poseidon   25
even as Klotho lifted him up from the   one of the Fates, at his birth
   cauldron of purity,
marked with a gleaming ivory shoulder.
Marvels are many and mortal reports
decked out with fanciful lies may sometimes
outpass the truth, to deceive a
   wondering listener.

2. Charis builds all that is sweet among men; she brings   Charis=grace/glory
   honor and
often she renders believable what should be   31
past all belief, though following days
make wiser witnesses.
Men should speak well of the gods—
this brings less blame. O son of Tantalos,   35
   spurning the old tales,
I shall recount how your father once
summoned the gods (as a
favor returned) to a tranquil
banquet at Sipylos, and how the
lord of the trident, mastered by lust,   40

carried you off, driving his golden team up to the high
palace of wide-ruling Zeus, where afterwards
Ganymede came, serving that lord in
similar fashion.
You disappeared, nor did men who made search bring you   45
home to your mother, and one of the
   envious neighbors
whispered of fire, limbs chopped by a
sharp blade into a
bubbling pot, and of guests at
table who, when the first course was gone,   50
portioned you out and devoured you.

ep. I cannot libel a god as greedy of gut—
   this I refuse to do!
Small profit comes to the man who speaks slander. If
ever the watchers of heaven
honored a mortal, that man was Tantalos, who   55
   failed to digest such great
bliss. His appetite won him an
unending doom when, over his head,
Zeus hung a threatening stone, that he—
straining to cast it away—should be
exiled forever from joy.

3. Such is the weary perpetual pain of his life, with a   fourth=immortality
fourth trial added to three, for he stole   three=hunger, thirst, apprehension
   from the
gods the ambrosia and nectar that   61
kept him from death, to
share it with drinking companions. He is in
error who thinks that a deed can ever be
   hidden from god.
Tantalos' son was sent back by the   65
deathless ones, down among
short-lived men, but when puberty
darkened his chin the lad thought of marriage—
that he might take, from her Pisan father,

Hippodameia, a girl much admired. He went down one   70
night to the edge of the white-flecked sea and
standing alone hailed the thunderous
god of the trident, who   *Poseidon*
faced him at once. Then the youth spoke: "If
love-gifts from Kypris brought pleasure to   75
   you, o Poseidon, then
ground Oinomaos' bronze spear and   *father of Hippodameia*
send me to Elis
driving the swiftest of cars—
equip me with strength! He has already slain
thirteen bold suitors to hold off the day of   80

ep. his daughter's wedding. Never do great risks
   seek out a coward.
Why should a man who must die ever huddle in shadow,
nameless and nursing a useless
old-age bereft of fine deeds? This
   contest awaits me—
give it the end I desire!" So he spoke,   85
nor were his words without fruit for the
god offered fame in the form of a chariot
all made of gold, with horses both
   winged and tireless.

4. He overtook the bold Oinomaos, bedded the girl and
by her engendered six sons, each eager for
valiant deeds. Now, reclining at   90
Alpheos' ford,
he knows the blood of glorious sacrifice
there in his visited tomb close by the
   altar that strangers seek.   *the great altar of Zeus*
Fame from Olympia, taken in
contests of swiftness and   95
painful endurance where Pelops once
raced, is seen from afar, and through all his
life the victor knows honey-sweet calm,

thanks to these games! Bliss that returns with each day is man's
finest possession. My given task is to   100
garland this man with Aiolic song
cast in equestrian
mode, for I know that no host of our
time is more lordly in strength and fair deeds, more
　　fit to be wrapped in the
folds of elaborate fame-bearing   105
hymns. O Hieron, a
god takes charge of your every ambition!
Let him not leave you and soon I shall sing
even more sweetly of your flying car,   Hieron's chariot won at Olympia in
                                                        468 but Pindar did not make the ode

ep. finding a friendly pathway of words as I   110
　　move beside Kronos'
sun-covered hill! The Muses' most powerful shafts are
nurtured for me. Men achieve
splendors of various sorts but ruling kings
　　stand at the peak. Look no
further! I beg you may walk on the heights through
all of your days, and that I, in my   115
time, may move among victors as
poetry's manifest light, visible
　　throughout all Hellas.

For Theron of Akragas, to celebrate a victory in the four-horse chariot race. Theron was son of Ainesidamos, brother of Xenokrates (see Pythian 6), and ruler of this wealthy city on the southern coast of Sicily from about 488 BC until his death in the late 470s; the family claimed descent from one of Oedipus' sons (lines 37–9). With Gelo of Syracuse, Theron defeated the Carthaginian fleet at Himera in 480 BC, and, as kin by marriage, he continued to be a close ally of Hieron.

    Akragas was the city of Empedokles, and this ode reflects local eschatological beliefs, as it offers the possibility of an eternal glory that would surpass even the good fame that poetry can give.
476 BC

1. You Hymns, lords of the lyre—what god, what
hero, what man shall we sing?
Pisa means Zeus, and the
    games at Olympia were
Herakles' trophy of war, while for the   cf. O. 10
victory won by his four-horse team   5
Theron must now be proclaimed! Due host to strangers,
    prop of Akragas, scion of glorious
forebears, he holds the city upright!

His race, much tried in spirit, conquered the
sacred riverbank site as   10
Sicily's eye and their
    fate added splendor and
wealth to strengths bred in the bone. Now,
o son of Rhea and Kronos,   Zeus
throned on Olympos, lord of the highest of contests at
    Alpheos' ford, be cheered by our songs and
guard, for descendants to come, these

ep. ancestral fields! What has been done,   15
whether in justice or wrongly, not even
Chronos the father of all can undo but,   Time
   with fortune's favor,
forgetfulness comes.
Pain dies, crushed beneath
joys that are noble, its evil defeated,   20

2. when divine Fate sends bliss to its heights!   Moira
This truth is proved by the
daughters of Kadmos:
   challenged by blessings more
powerful, heaviest grief may subside!
Long-haired Semelē died by the fiery   mother of Dionysos
bolt but now lives with Olympians, cherished by   26
   Muses, Pallas and Zeus, and
loved beyond all by her ivy-crowned son!

Men say that Ino, deep in the sea, is
granted an unchanging life as
timeless companion to   30
   Nereus' sea-dwelling
daughters. For mortals the border of death is
not known, nor do we finish one single
day (each a child of the sun) in tranquility,
   blessings undamaged. Men are engulfed in
uncertain floods of pleasure and pain.

ep. So Moira, as she maintains the familial   cf. above, line 21
fate of these men, will sometimes bring grief to   36
mingle with festival joy, then turn it away.
   This she has done since
Laios' doomed son encountered his   Oedipus
father and killed him, true to the
Pythian oracles heard long before.   40

3. A sharp-eyed Erinys saw and brought   an avenging power
death to his warrior sons through   Eteokles and Polyneikes

mutual slaughter, yet
    when Polyneikes had
fallen, Thersander lived on, to be honored in   his son
contests of boys, then in war—a rescuing   45
son for the house of Adrastos. Sprung from such seed,
    Ainesidamos' son now rightly
meets with sung praises and tones of the lyre.

He took the prize at Olympia, while at
Delphi and Isthmia the fine
fortune they share gave his   50
    brother a flowering   Xenokrates, cf. P. 6, l. 2
crown from the twelve-lap chariot trial.
Contest success brings escape from care.
Wealth, when inwrought with virtue, opens up
    many a chance and strengthens a
deep ferocious ambition. It is a

ep. far-shining star, truest of lights,   55
if he who holds it knows what will come: how
each helpless heart, as it dies, pays an immediate
    penalty, then—for   for an existential crime? cf. fr. 133SM
crimes performed here in the realm of
Zeus—meets an underground   59
judge whose words hold a hateful necessity.   below, line 76

4. Through nights ever equal and equal days
good men are given a life without
toil, never troubling the
    earth with rude hands, never
ploughing the sea for its spare sustenance.
Those who rejoice in keeping their   65
oaths find a tearless existence, led in the
    presence of gods highly honored, while   Hades and Persephonē
others know agonies past contemplation.

All who endure three terms in both realms,   three in all or three on each side?
souls free from injustice, follow the

highway of Zeus to the   70
    tower of Kronos where
soft ocean winds breathe round the Isles of the
Blest. There petals of gold blaze,
some from bright trees on the shore, some rising
    up from the water, and these they
twist into bracelets and crowns, for

ep. such is the will of the upright   75
judge, Rhadamanthys, seated forever
with the great father, husband of high-throned   Kronos
    Rhea. Lords Kadmos and
Peleus dwell in this place
and too Achilles, brought by his
mother, whose prayers had moved Zeus. He   80

5. overthrew Hektor, unshakable pillar of
Troy; brought death as well to
Kyknos and Dawn's
    Ethiope son! Many swift   son=Memnon
arrows still rest in the quiver under my
elbow, ready to speak to the knowing (the   85
mob will need an interpreter). Wise is the
    man who knows much by nature;
those needing lessons gabble like crows that

caw at the sacred eagle of Zeus! Come, take
aim, o my soul! Whom shall we
strike as with gentle intent we   90
    let fly our fame-bearing
shafts? Stretching my bow toward Akragas,
my mind set upon truth, I swear that
no other city in one hundred years has
    bred up a lord more ready to succor his
friends, less stingy of hand than is

ep. Theron! But close upon praise   95
noxious satiety follows, not with

justice but fostered by envious men who would
   hide the fair deeds of the
noble in babbling slander.
Sea-sands are numberless, and too his
gifts of generous joy—who could count them?   100

OLYMPIAN 3   Herakles and the Olive Trees

Again celebrating Theron of Akragas for his chariot victory of 476 BC (cf. Olympian 2), this song seems to be meant for performance during a ritual banquet to which gods and heroes (Herakles, Kastor, and Pollux) are invited as guests (lines 39–41).

The ruler who brings the glory of an Olympic crown to his city is set beside the Herakles who brought the shade of the first olive to Olympia. Restored to chronological order, the mythic events revived by the song come in this sequence: (1) Herakles' pursuit of the hind of Taÿgeta (the Third Labor) and his first glimpse of northern olive trees (lines 26–32); (2) Herakles' establishment of games at Olympia and his memory of the trees (lines 19–25, 33–4); (3) the hero's journey to the Hyperboreans to beg for trees (lines 16, 25–6); (4) his return with the first Olympian olive wreath (line 14).

The background story concerned the nymph, Taÿgeta, who was pursued by Zeus and transformed by Artemis into a hind. When she was finally taken, she returned the hind to the goddess, inscribing one of its golden horns with her dedication (line 30), but the creature escaped from the temple precinct, to be returned by Herakles only after a long pursuit commanded by Eurystheus (line 28).

476 BC

1. I aim to please the guest-loving Tyndarids,   Kastor and Pollux (cf. N. 10)
     golden-haired Helen, too,
while I pay honor to famous Akragas and
rouse up for Theron the hymn of Olympian victory
     owed to the tireless
hooves of his team! Once more the Muse
     stands at my side as I search out a
new-fashioned mix of Dorian dance with   5

voices that celebrate triumph. Crowns
     fixed in my hair mark a

21

ritual duty of joining the elegant
tones of the lyre with a shout from the pipe and a pattern of
   words in due praise of
Hagesidamos' brave son, and
   Pisa commands me as well. Songs   Olympia
travel from there, god-sent and destined for   10

ep. him on whose brow the strict Elian judge,
following Herakles' ancient rule,
   places a wreath of gray olive to
bind in his hair—leaves from the tree
   brought long ago by Amphitryon's
son from the shadowy sources of   by Herakles from the Danube
   Ister to serve as best
emblem of games at Olympia, once his   15

2. words had persuaded the men of Apollo who
   live beyond Boreas.   home of the north wind
He made his plea in good faith, wanting a
tree for the famed grove of Zeus, as shade to be shared by the
   crowd, and as a badge of
valiant success. His father's altars once
   hallowed, the eye of the midmonth
moon had shone full upon him from her golden   20

car as on Alpheos' banks he established a sacred
   judging of games and a
festival, every four years, but no splendid
trees as yet grew in that field by the Kronian Hill—
   Pelops' domain. To him the
precinct seemed naked, enslaved to the sharp
   rays of the sun, and in that
moment his heart had urged him to go   25

ep. back to the Istrian land where Orthosia,   Artemis
horse-driving daughter of Leto, had
   earlier met him, come from Arkadia's
ridges and glens, forced by Eurystheus

(and by the oath of his father) to
bring back the hind whose horns were of
    gold, the gift that Taÿgeta
offered to Artemis with her inscription.   30

3. Chasing that doe, he'd glimpsed the land that lies
    back of the chill winds of
Boreas and he had stood there in silence,
stunned by the trees. A sweet longing to plant just such
    trees at the turn of his twelve-lap
course later seized him, and now he is
    glad as he visits that Elean
festival, joining the twin sons of Leda!   Kastor and Pollux

To them, when he went to Olympos, he left the   36
    care of his glorious
contests of muscle and chariot skills.
My heart commands me say that these same horse-loving
    Tyndarids now bring
glory to Theron and to the Emmenid tribe,
    who, of all men, have most frequently
welcomed these heroes at their friendly feasts,   40

ep. piously keeping the rites of the Blessed. If
water is best, gold the most honored of
    all man's possessions, so it is
Theron who reaches the outermost
    edge of success, moving from home to
Herakles' pillars! No wise man goes
    further, nor even the
unwise. I'll not attempt it—I'd be a fool!   45

OLYMPIAN 4   A Gray Haired Victor

For Psaumis of Kamarina, a city on the southeastern coast of Sicily (destroyed by Gelo in 485 BC but rebuilt in 461 BC). The victory has been taken with the unpretentious mule cart, and not by a member of a ruling family, so the song is modest. The closing reference to the "grey hairs of Erginos" (lines 20 ff.) reminds the audience of the voyage of the Argonauts while it also suggests that Psaumis has reached middle age. 460 or 456 BC

1. Zeus, supreme driver of tireless thunder, the
   Horai, your daughters who dance in a   goddesses of the seasons
circle to intricate tunes from the lyre,
send me as witness to tell of the proudest of contests!
When friends succeed men who are noble
show prompt delight at the news, and so may you,   5
o son of Kronos and ruler of Aitna where Typhon's
hundred rough heads lie trapped beneath   cf. P. 1.15–20
   wind-blasted heights. For the sake of the Graces
welcome this revel that celebrates
victory won at Olympia—a long-lasting

light that rests upon deeds of broad strength! It   10
   touches the mule-cart of Psaumis who,
crowned with the olive of Pisa, hastens to
spur Kamarina's renown. May some kindly god
favor his prayers in the future!
I praise him now as skilled in the schooling of
horses and happy to welcome all guests to his   15
table, a pure-minded servant of
   Quietude, she who is friend to all cities.   Hesychia, cf. P. 8.1–18
I will not stain my speech with a lie: among
men, proof comes with trial—such

ep. trial as freed Klymenos' son from the   Erginos, an Argonaut
   scorn of the Lemnian women.   cf. P. 4.252–3
   Taking his crown from Hypsipylē's hands   21
   after the heavy-armed race, he announced,
"Such as I am in swiftness of foot
   so am I also in hand and in heart!
   Grey hairs may grow from the heads of
   young men before the appointed time."

Again for Psaumis of Kamarina. The occasion seems to be the same as for Olympian 4, and some have supposed that two sons of the victor each commissioned an ode; others, finding Olympian 5 to be beneath Pindar's usual poetic level, have attributed it to a Sicilian imitator. The singers refer (lines 8, 13–14) to the rebuilding of Kamarina, completed in 461–460 BC, and they also report that Psaumis has competed at some time with a single horse and with a chariot team (line 7).
460 or 456 BC

1. Take the sweet bloom of Olympian crowns and high
courage, o daughter of Ocean, for these are the gifts   daughter=Kamarina
brought you by Psaumis and by his tireless mules!

He, Kamarina, exalted your nurturing city when at the
gods' greatest feast he honoured the six double altars with   5
ox-blood, and in the five days of contest with

ep. mules, chariots, and racing steeds! To you his victory
gave sweet renown when, after Akron his father, the
    herald named your new-built site!

2. O Pallas guardian of cities, he comes from the fair fields of
Pelops and lord Oinomaos, praising your undefiled   10
grove, the river Oanos, your nearby lake, and the

hallowed canals that let Hipparis answer the thirst of the
people and build a high forest of dwellings, raising the
men of this city from helplessness into the light!

ep. Here, toil and expense ever strive toward deeds hidden in   15
danger, and those who succeed are thought wise
    even by their fellow townsmen.   i.e., there is no envy here

26

3. O savior Zeus, cloud-high keeper of Kronos' hill, patron of
Alpheos' streams and of Ida's most holy cave, I come as a
suppliant breathing through Lydian flutes to

beg that you grant to this city deeds of famed prowess as   20
ornaments. For our Olympian victor—o Psaumis, for
you—I ask a life lived to a spirited end,

ep. cheered by the teams of Poseidon, surrounded by sons! If a man
keeps his wealth sound, to sufficiency adding good fame,
    let him not seek to be god!

OLYMPIAN 6   The Birth of Iamos

For Hagesias, a citizen of Syracuse in Sicily and victor in the mule-cart race. Hagesias, a young (line 76 notes his beauty) associate of the Syracusan tyrant Hieron (lines 93–9), was a member of the Iamid clan, a Lakedaimonian family that had supplied prophets and seers to various Greek places, including Olympia, for several centuries. The Syracusan branch was closely connected with other descendants of Iamos located in the Arkadian city of Stymphalos (lines 76–84), and the victor's party seems to have gone from Olympia to that place for a preliminary celebration before returning to Syracuse for a second performance (lines 96–101). With them they evidently brought a certain Aineias (lines 88–92), who carried the text of the ode and supervised the dancers; at line 81 he is addressed by the singers as if their voice were that of Pindar (for similar sung instructions to a chorus leader, see the end of Isthmian 2). Note the pretense that an Arkadian audience might consider a song made at Thebes to be countrified (line 89).
468 BC

1. Pillars of gold we shall raise,
     as for the well-built porch of a
splendid abode, for our song,
as it begins, needs a façade that
shines from afar! If a man be Olympian victor,
     guardian at Pisa of
Zeus' oracular shrine, and one of the   5
founders of famed Syracuse, what
     praise can he hope to escape as he
moves among townsmen not
     stingy with much-desired song?

Let Sostratos' son understand—
     his foot fits this shoe! Fine deeds
done without risk, whether on

land or at sea, go without honor but   IO
when a high task is painfully finished, many
   remember. Hagesias,
fitting to you is the praise that Adrastos' tongue   Argive leader at Thebes
shaped for Amphiaraos the
   Oikleid prophet,
as, with his shining team, earth
seized him and swallowed him down.   cf. N. 9.24–7

ep. When seven pyres had consumed their dead   15
   these words were spoken at
Thebes by Talaos' son: "I long for the   son=Adrastos
   eye of my army, best
prophet and best at wielding a spear!"
   Just such a one is this man,   Hagesias
master of revels, come out from Syracuse—
I don't seek quarrels, nor am I
victory-mad but to this I will swear a great   20
oath, while the honey-voiced Muses
   lend their support!

2. Come Phintis, yoke your strong mules—   Hagesias' driver
   do it with speed!—that we may
drive our cart forth on an open
path and arrive at the root of this
family. Your team knows, better than all, how to   25
   travel this road, having
taken Olympian crowns. Hymn-gates must open to
them, for today we shall follow the
   river Eurotas as far as   river in Lakedaimon
Pitana, that we may   town on the Eurotas, near Sparta
   reach that fair place in good time!

She, so men say, couched by the   the nymph Pitana
   Kronian Poseidon, carried a
child, the dark-haired Evadnē, but   30
being unwed she veiled her womb's pain,
then at the birth-month ordered her servants to give the babe

into the care of
Eilatos' son, who on Alpheos' banks   son=Aipytos
ruled the Arkadians of Phaisana.
    Fostered there, she first
touched Aphrodite's sweet   35
    gifts with Apollo as guide.

ep. Nor could the god's seed be hidden from
    Aipytos. His heart's
anger made dumb by a sharper concern, he
    journeyed to Pytho
with his unbearable pain, that he might
    hear the advice of the god.
Soon she loosened her purple sash, put down her
silver jar under a hedge and gave birth to a   40
god-inspired boy, while to attend her the
golden-haired god sent Fates and the
    mild Eleithyia.   the birth goddess

3. He, Iamos, came from her womb
    into the light with a swift, sweet
pang and, weeping, she left him
there on the ground, where by the gods' will   45
two green-eyed snakes nursed him with innocent venom
    made by the bees. The
king, come back from steep Pytho, questioned his
household concerning a child lately
    born to Evadnē—a
boy, so he said, who was
fathered by Phoibos and fated to

be, of all mortals, the greatest of   50
    prophets, nor would his line ever fail.
Such were his words, but all swore that
no one had seen or heard of a five-day old
babe, though in truth he lay hidden, deep in a
    dense bed of bracken, his
tender flesh bathed in shafts of rich purple and

gold that fell from the violets there,   55
   giving his mother the
undying name that she
   chose to be his for all time—

ep. Iamos! When gold-crowned Hebē had   *ia*=violet / *ios*=venom
   given her fruit, he
went one night down to the Alpheos, stood
   midstream out under the
sky, and called to Poseidon, his mother's
   father and also to
him whose bow protects Delos the god-built   Apollo
isle. When he asked for the care of a people the   61
clear, close voice of his father made answer:
"Rise, child, and follow my words to a
   land shared by all!"

4. They came in time to the steep hill of
   Kronos where the god
granted him two stores of prophecy: 65
first, a voice in his ear, untouched by
falsehood; and second, when Herakles, Alkaios'
   offshoot, should boldly
invent for his father a holiday feast and the   i.e., his real father, Zeus
best of all organized games, he was—   cf. O. 10.44–77
   by the god's order—to set up his
own mantic shrine at the   70
   summit of Zeus' great altar.

Since then the fame of the Iamid
   race spreads among Hellenes.
Riches pursue them while they, as
every deed proves, follow an open path,
honoring valor, yet envious blame ever
   waits upon those who
win on the twelve-lap course, when   75
Charis drips glorious beauty upon them. If
   your mother's kin, o Hagesias,

men who reside on the
    slopes of Kyllenē, have   *in Arkadia*

ep. piously offered up victims and prayers to
    Hermes, as heavenly
Herald, keeper of prizes and games and the
    power who honors
Arkadian courage, then it must be he, o   80
    son of Sostratos, who with his
thundering father decrees your success! I   *father=Zeus*
feel on my tongue a shrill whetstone and
welcome its flood of sweet breath for my mother's
mother was Stymphalian too—Metopē,
    flowering nymph whose   *singers speak for their Theban poet*

5. daughter was horse-driving Thebē! I   85
    drink her pure water, while for these
spearmen I weave an elaborate hymn.
Rouse up your comrades, Aineas, first to sing   *leader of the chorus*
Hera the Virgin, then to learn whether with   *a Stymphalian cult*
    words of truth we can
cheat the old taunt of "Boiotian pig!"—
you, the envoy of lovely-haired Muses, their   90
    rod of remembrance and
sweet mixing-bowl for
    echoing full-voiced songs!

Tell them to sing of Ortygia and
    Syracuse, city where Hieron
rules, wise in counsel, his scepter unstained.
He serves the red-shod Demeter, keeps the
feast of the maid of white steeds, and honors the power of   95
    Aitnaian Zeus. Melodies   *maid of white steeds=Persephonē*
know him, and sweet-speaking lyres! Let oncoming
time not trouble his bliss, and may he
    welcome Hagesias' reveling
band with gestures of cordial good-
    fellowship as it arrives,

ep. come home from home after leaving the
   walls of Stymphalos,
mother of sheep-filled Arkadia. Cast from a   100
   swift-moving ship on a
storm-filled night of midwinter, two
   anchors are best. May some
favoring god send glory to both!   Syracuse and Stymphalos
Lord of the sea, spouse of a   spouse=Poseidon; goddess=Amphitritē
    goddess whose
spindle is gold, grant a voyage both carefree and
short and strengthen the joyous   105
   bloom of my songs!

OLYMPIAN 7 A Snowstorm of Gold

For Diagoras of Rhodes, son of Damagetos of the Eratid tribe, victor in boxing. Diagoras was the heaviest and most successful boxer of his time, with prizes from all four crown contests, and his two sons were also Olympic victors. Such marked success might attract some sudden reversal, so the song ends with a formal assertion of the uncertainty of mortal fortunes (lines 94–5).

The song's mythic events go back to the beginning of the Olympian order; in chronological order they are (1) the portioning of the earth among the sons of Kronos, with Rhodes granted to Helios and at once populated with sons and grandsons of the god and the island nymph (lines 54–74); (2) the birth of Athena from the head of Zeus, the failed sacrifice, and the golden snow, which conferred skill in the art of statue making (with perhaps a jibe at the Telchines, earlier sea-demon craftsmen, lines 34–53); (3) the murder of an uncle, committed at Tiryns by Herakles' son, Tlepolemos, and his subsequent settlement on Rhodes (lines 27–33); (4) the founding of Rhodian games to honor Tlepolemos (lines 77–80).
464 BC

1. As with a lavish hand a man takes a cup
foaming with wine, sips, and offers it—
wealth's golden summit—
to a young son-in-law, hearth to
    hearth, adding grace to the
banquet and honoring his new kin,   5
    making him envied by friends for a
marriage of like with like—just so do I

offer poured nectar, sweet fruit of the mind and
gift of the Muses, to men who take
prizes at Pytho   Delphi
or at Olympia! Blessed is   10

34

he whom fair report
seizes. Charis, the giver of bloom,
    favors one, then another, as
musical strings join the babbling pipe.

ep. Now as I come with Diagoras
    both sounds are heard!
I sing of Rhodes, born from the sea,
    daughter of Kypris and Helios' bride,
that I may praise this giant contender,   15
    paying the wage of one who's been
crowned for his boxing at Delphi
and at the Alpheos. I shall sing too of his   Olympia
    sire, Damagetos, beloved of justice, for both
dwell on this isle of three cities near Asia's   Rhodes
coast, with spearmen from Argos as neighbors.

2. I shall begin with Tlepolemos as I   20
make their tale known, for as members of
Herakles' powerful race
they claim descent from Zeus on the
    father's side and are
kin to Amyntor through Astydameia.
    Errors hang numberless over men's
thoughts, and none can discover what may be   25

best for a man to attain, now and in the
end. At Tiryns, in anger, a man took his
olive-wood sceptre to
murder Likymnios, Alkmena's
    brother come back from Midea—the
man was Tlepolemos, this island's   30
    founder! Storms strike even the
minds of the wise. He consulted the god,

ep. and from his incense-filled cell the
    golden-haired one   Apollo
spoke of a voyage out from the

rough cliffs of Lerna and over to
this sea-girt land where the king of the
    gods once buried a city in
deep golden snow—this when with   35
help from Hephaistos' skilled axe Athena had
    leapt from the summit of her father's head, her
battle-cry causing the heavens to shudder while
Ge, the earth's mother, shuddered as well.

3. Helios, light-giving child of Hyperion, had
then set a task for his sons to fulfill—   cf. line 71
they should be first to   41
raise up an altar for this new
    divinity, where they might
gladden both father and spear-wielding maid with   Zeus and Athena
    sacrifice. Awe, child of
forethought brings courage and joy, but a strange

cloud of forgetting may settle on men, to   45
hide the straight path from their minds. So these
islanders went up,
    carrying no seed of flame!
    Their lofty precinct was
founded with rites that lacked fire, but Zeus yet
    sent down upon them a cloud that rained
copious gold, while Athena, the grey-eyed   50

ep. goddess, gave into their hands a surpassing
    skill in all crafts. Soon
statues like animate creatures
    stood on their streets, giving them fame.
Where men are wise, art wrought without
    guile has the greater effect.   ref. to local magicians, the Telchines?
Legends from long ago tell that when
Zeus, with the other immortals, shared out the   55
    earth, Rhodes was not to be seen on the
broad sea's surface but rested below,
hidden in those salty depths, nor was

4. Helios present. No lot fell to him, no
portion of earth, though he was a
sacred divinity.   60
Zeus, once reminded, offered to
   make a new cast but the
other refused, for he had perceived, growing
   up from the floor of the sea, a land
fruitful for men and kindly to grazing sheep.

He bade Lachesis the gold-crowned to   one of the Fates
lift up her hands and, true to the   65
gods' solemn oath,
join Kronos' son in granting this
   land—once risen and
visible in the bright air—to him, to be
   his for all time. And the
thrust of his words became truth, for there

ep. grew up from the sea the island now held by the   70
   father of sharp shafts of
light, the master of fire-breathing steeds. With
   Rhodes as his bride he sired seven sons,
their minds far wiser than those of the
   children of men. One of these
fathered three brothers—Kamiros,
Lindos, and Ialysos the eldest—
   princes who then divided their
heritage, fixing three parts and each taking a   75
city soon to be called by his name.

5. There a sweet retribution for bitter misfortune is
made to Tlepolemos, founder from Tiryns, as
if to a god—sheep
moving toward sacrifice, then that   80
   judging of athletic
trials where Diagoras twice wore a flowery crown. At
   Isthmia he had four victories,
many again at Nemea and rocky Athens.

Known to the bronze shield at Argos and to the tripods of
Thebes and Arkadia, he gained prizes as well at
games in Boiotia   85
and too in Pellana. Six times a
   victor at Aigina,
this same number is wrought in Megarian stone.
   O father Zeus, Atabyrion's lord,   mountain on Rhodes
honor the custom of victory song and

ep. honor this man who invented the
   virtue of fists!
Grant him reverent thanks from   90
   strangers and townsmen for, taught by the
right-thinking minds of his ancestors, he takes the
   path that shuns arrogance.
Do not obscure this seed they have
shared since the epoch of Kallianax! When   ancestor of the Diagoras
   Eratids celebrate triumphs the city holds
festival too. Still, winds as they shift may in
one single moment whirl this way and that.   95

For Alkimedon of the island of Aigina, victor in the boys' wrestling, son
of Iphion (now dead, line 81), grandson of Timosthenes (lines 15, 70),
and probably nephew of the Kallimachos who is with Iphion in Hades
(line 82). The Blepsiads of line 75 are the victor's tribe. The grandfather,
Timosthenes, had been a victor at Nemea, and it was probably he who
commissioned the present ode.

Aiakos, son of Zeus and Aigina, was the hero most honored on this is-
land; the reference to his first and third generations (lines 45–6) points to
his son Telamon, who fought in the first Trojan War, and to his great-
grandson, Neoptolemos, Achilles' son, who was prominent in the second.

The praise of the trainer Melesias (lines 54–66) is the most extensive
of all such passages, and one may note the pretense that other trainers
may be envious (line 55).
460 BC

1. Mother of gold-crowned games and mistress of
truth—Olympia, where men of prophesy
judge fiery trials to discover from
    Zeus of the shining bolt
what he intends for those who
deep in their hearts are eager to   5
seize upon valor, then
take a new breath, recovered from toil!

Achievement is piety's recompense. O
grove by the Alpheos, well-wooded Pisa,
welcome this crown-bearing band! Where   10
    your bright prize goes
fame ever follows, yet
various goods come to various
men and, with heaven's aid,
more than one path can lead to success.

ep. Your clan, Timosthenes, fate gave to Zeus, its   15
ancestral god; at Nemea he honored you and now by the
Kronian hill at Olympia he grants a crown to Alkimedon!
Handsome to look at, his deeds did not sully his
form when, best in the ring, he named
Aigina as his homeland, famed for her   20
   long oars, island where
Themis the savior, throne-mate of
Zeus lord of strangers, is cherished with

2. honors unique among men. Where much
hangs in an unsteady balance, judgement
both fair and apt is hard to pin down   a wrestling term is used
   but by a law of the
gods this island is fixed as a   26
magical pillar for strangers from   a sanctuary
all lands—may dawning
time never tire of supporting a land

laid up as treasure for Dorian people since   30
Aiakos' day! Mighty Poseidon and
Leto's child summoned that hero to   child=Apollo
   Troy to help them as
they began work on its circlet of
walls, for fate had decreed an
onrush of war for that place—   35
battles and belchings of turbulent smoke.

ep. Citadel built, three pale snakes leapt against it,
two to fall back and die, terror-struck, while the third gave a
shout and flung itself over the wall. Apollo pondered the
unfriendly omen, then plainly cried out,   40
"Troy will be taken where your hand, o
hero, has worked—so speaks this vision
   sent here by thundering
Zeus, son of Kronos—nor,
apart from your children, shall these walls be

3. breached. They will fall with the first and the   45
third generations." Plainly he spoke, then
drove off toward Xanthos, Ister and
      Amazon lands, while the
lord of the trident turned his swift
car toward the Isthmian bridge
(his golden team bringing   50
Aiakos here on the way), that he might   here=Aigina

view his Korinthian feast-grounds. No   site of the Isthmian games
joy among mortals can ever be equal to
this! If my song takes a turn toward the   this=driving in a god's chariot
      fame that Melesias
won among boys, let envy not   55
cast its rough stones, for I say he knew the
same joy at Nemea, then,
among men, took the prize in the

ep. pankration! One who knows teaches easily;
not to foresee is foolish and hearts yet untried are too   60
eager. This man, better than any, could foretell a contest,
knowing the style that would further an
athlete determined to take from the
sacred games what he most longed for—
      fame. Now to this
trainer Alkimedon brings a   65
thirtieth victory prize! With

4. god-given luck but true to his own inner strength
he forced a hateful return on the limbs of
four other boys. Scorned, they came
      dodging up hidden back
alleys while into his grandsire   70
he breathed a force that wrestles with age.
Practicing timely rites, a   rites such as victory celebrations
man may forget about Hades! Still,

I must awaken remembrance, announcing this
triumph of hands to the Blepsiads—they may now   75
circle their brows with a sixth crown
    taken at games that give
garlands! Even the dead are
granted a share in well-observed rituals—
dust cannot hide the prized
festival joy of a kinsman.   80

ep. Learning from Angel, the daughter of Hermes,
Iphion might turn to Kallimachos, naming this shining
crown from Olympia granted to their line by Zeus. May he
choose to pile others on these noble gifts
and may he banish sharp woe! I pray he will
not, to their portion of blessings, add a   85
    two-minded Nemesis—   i.e., a mixed fate
I ask that he raise up this clan and this city,
bringing them life without pain!

The Flood

For Epharmostos of Opous in Eastern Lokris beneath Parnassos; victor in wrestling, Epharmostos has already won at Delphi, Isthmia, Nemea, Marathon, Thebes, and Eleusis, as well as in various Arkadian contests (lines 82–100). For some reason neither father nor tribe is named for this victor, and the only ancestors claimed are Zeus, Titans, and the Stone People created by Deukalion and Pyrrha after the flood had devastated the earth and its inhabitants (line 46). The central mythic event (lines 57–65) demonstrates how these three strains were mixed when a child sired by Zeus upon a granddaughter of the Titan Deukalion (daughter of Opous, line 57) became the first ruler of Lokris, a city of Stone People.

The Lampromachos named in line 83 was identified by ancient scholiasts as a relative, but the song implies that he was an outsider with special status at Opous, and the Patroklos digression (lines 69–79) suggests that he was a favorite companion of the victor; the tone of the introductory Herakles example (29–35) gives the rest of the song the flavor of spirited youth.
466 BC

1. The Archilochos chant—
"Victor triumphant!"
      shouted three times—could
open the revels when, close by the
Kronian hill, Epharmostos danced with his   at Olympia
friends but today a volley of far-flying   5
shafts like these must sweep from the
bows of the Muses, targeting Zeus,
lord of red lightning, and too his sacred
Elian peak, fairest of dowries given to
Lydian Pelops when Hippodameia was won!   cf. O. 1.65–89

Send off a sweet feathered   II
shaft against Pytho!
    Words won't fall short as your
harp makes its circle to honor a
son of famed Opous for skill in the ring. Praise the
man and the city allotted to   14
Themis and savior Eunomia, her   cosmic order / respect for law
child! At your spring, Kastalia, she   she=Opous
blooms with fine deeds, and beside Alpheos
where finest crowns raise this tree-shaded
city, mother of Lokrian men, into fame.   20

ep. I shall ignite blazing songs to illumine a
city well loved, sending my message in
every direction faster than
any prize steed or ship under sail,
if to my work in the   25
    Graces' best garden
I bring a destined skill!
Joy is their gift but men become
    noble or wise only as some

2. power divine may decree.
How else at Pylos could   30
    Herakles brandish his
club when hard-pressed by Poseidon or
under attack by the silver bow of Apollo,
or when Hades made generous use of the
rod that drives corpses down to the
echoing streets of the dying? But, o my mouth,   35
spit out that tale! Casting the gods in
scandalous roles is a skill to be hated, and
loud boasts, made out of season, harmonize

only with madness.
Scorn such fools' talk—   40
    leave war and violence
far from the gods as your tongue now

touches the city of Protogeneia! There
by the order of thundering Zeus, Deu-   Hesiod *Cat.* 2–7
kalion and Pyrrha made their first
home and with no act of love founded a   45
race made from pebbles called People of Stone.
Open a pathway of verses for them—praise
old wine but songs of a more recent vintage!

ep. Men still tell of a watery deluge that
flooded the black earth, and of a sudden   50
ebb-tide of Zeus' contrivance that
drained off the land. Then from Deukalion and
Pyrrha your ancestors came,
    armed youths born to the
daughters of Iapetos' race and to   Titans
Kronos' magnificent sons.   Olympians
    They ruled as native-born kings

3. 'til the Olympian lord
snatched up the daughter of
    Opous from Elis,
couched her in secret on Mainolos'
slopes, then brought her to Lokros lest that man should   60
end his days childless. She held the
most sacred seed and the king looked with
joy on the son he was given, naming him
after the mother's sire, that as a man   sire=Opous
he might be wondrous in form and in deeds, and he   65
gave him the rule of the People of Stone and their city.

From Pisa and Thebes,
Arkadia and Argos,
    friends came to join him   the second Opous, come of age
but to Menoitios he gave most
honor, the son fathered by Aktor on Aigina.   70
His son in turn, gone with the Atreids
out to the Mysian plain, was the
one man to stand by Achilles when

Telephos routed the valorous Greeks and   cf. I. 5.41, 8.55
threatened their ships—proof to a sensible man of the   75
fierce will of Patroklos. That was when Thetis' son   Achilles

ep. ordered him never to stand apart when
furious Ares was near but to stay
close to his man-killing lance.
As I search for fit words, let me be   80
lifted away in the car of the
    Muses—may daring and
skill follow me! For friendship and
deeds I honor Lampromachos
    and for his Isthmian crown

4. taken when both men were   Lampromachos and Epharmostos
victors on one single   86
    day. Two further joys
touched Epharmostos at Korinth, a
third in the Nemean vale. At Argos he
won among men, at Athens
classed as a boy, and think of that   90
silver-cup contest at Marathon when,
barred from the beardless, he faced his elders and,
unthrown, took them with tricks! He earned such
shouts—young, fair and the doer of deeds yet more fair!

Wondrous was he when   95
all the Parrhasians
    gathered to celebrate   in Arkadia
Lykaian Zeus, and too at Pellana—
taking the prize that eases chill dawn! From his   prize=a cloak
tomb Iolaos could witness his glory   at Thebes
as did Eleusis, beside the sea.   100
Everywhere, what comes by nature is strongest.
Many seek fame with skills they have learned but
actions achieved where god is not present
suffer no damage when greeted with silence.

ep. Some roads lead further than others, nor does a   105
single ambition feed all. Steep is the
path of the arts but now, as you offer this prize, be
bold—shout it straight out, for
this man was born by god's will with
    hands full of strength, feet
able, and eyes brave! Now at the feast of   110
Oilias' son, as victor he places a   son=the lesser Ajax, the local hero
    crown on the altar of Ajax!

For Hagesidamos of Western Lokris in South Italy, son of Archestratos
and victor in boys' boxing. The reference to Ganymede (line 105) sug-
gests that Hagesidamos was entering the class of 15 to 19 year olds; cer-
tainly, the Ilas of line 18 is his trainer.

According to legend, when King Augeas of Elis refused to pay Her-
akles for cleaning his stables (the Tenth Labor), that hero brought an
army but was attacked and defeated by a force organized by the king's
nephews, the Moliones (sons of Poseidon sometimes represented as Sia-
mese twins). In return, Herakles killed them, attacking from ambush,
destroyed Augeas' kingdom, and then used its spoils to establish games
at Olympia.

The opening lines, with line 85, say that the ode has been delayed in
its delivery, while lines 8–12 suggest that in recompense Pindar has
made it longer that his commission required.
Ca. 476 BC

1. Read out the name of one crowned at Olympia, the
son of Archestratos—here, where it's
writ in my mind, for I promised sweet
    song, then forgot! O Muse,
join Alatheia the daughter of Zeus and   Truth
hold up your hand to protect me from untrue   5
charges of injury done to a friend!

Time that was future has come bringing shame for
my heavy debt. Still, here among men
interest added dissolves sharpest blame.
    See how the oncoming wave
swallows the tumbling pebble?—just   10
so shall we meet this old score, increasing our
payment with sweet gifts offered to friends.

ep. Rectitude rules in Zephyrian Lokris
where with Kalliopē bronze-armored Ares is
dear to all men. In combat with Kyknos   *thieving son of Ares*
    even strong Herakles turned. Let
Hagesidamos, Olympian victor in boxing,   16
offer his best thanks to Ilas
as, to Achilles, Patroklos did.
One man, by sharpening
natural valor, may, with god's   20
help, turn another toward
    gigantic glory.

2. Few, without labor, can capture the joy that
shines as life's beacon. Zeus' decrees
urge us to sing of the six-trial
    contest that Herakles
set at the archaic gravesite of Pelops   25
after he'd slain the sons of Poseidon,
unblemished Kteatos, Eurytos too,   *the twin Moliones*

that he might force from an unwilling Augeas
wages owed for his menial service.
He had hidden himself at Kleonai to   30
    ambush that pair on the
road because of his own Tirynthian army,
formerly camped in the lowlands of Elis
but there surprised and destroyed by the

ep. arrogant Moliones. And truly that
Epeian ruler, betrayer of guests, did   *ruler=Augeas*
afterward watch as his prospering fatherland   36
    sank in a pit of disaster—his
home-city lost to merciless fire and sharp iron blades.
Strife with a mightier foe
is not easy to end and that foolish
king, having fought to the   40
last was then captured, nor

did he escape death's
   steep sudden fall.

3. Zeus' brave son then gathered his host with   son=Herakles
all of its spoils into Pisa and
there for his most mighty father he   45
   measured a sacred grove,
fenced in the Altis as holy, and fixed the en-   the inner precinct
circling plain as a haven for feasts, with due
honors for Alpheos' ford and for the

twelve ruling gods. He saluted the hill of   the Olympians
Kronos, formerly nameless, where   50
during the reign of king Oinomaos   cf. O. 1.70–89
   thick snow would fall. In these
opening rites the Moirai stood close by his side,
as did that which alone, by its trials, can
find out and verify genuine truth—

ep. Time! This Power in his progress has clearly recorded   55
how as he portioned the profits of war he   he=Herakles
offered the best part to Zeus, then
   founded a four-year festival,
setting the first Olympian games with their prizes of
victory. Who then took a
new crown, striving with hands, with   60
feet or with chariot,
fixing in mind a vow of success,
then with his action
   making it real?

4. Best in the stadium race, running the
straight stretch on foot, was Oionos,   200 yards
son of Likymnios, come leading his   66
   host from Midea. In
wrestling, Echemos glorified Tegea; for
Tiryns, Doryklos won in the ring, and
from Mantinea came Samos to take the

four-horse chariot race—Halirothios'   70
son. Phrastor struck home with his lance and
Nikeus took the stone discus,
whirled it and sent it
furthest while unruly shouts burst from his
friends. In the evening the fair-faced moon
shed her beloved light and the   75

ep. whole sacred glade in glad celebration
feasted and sang as victors still do! True to these
ancient beginnings we'll chant that same hymn,
    named for proud victory, giving our   victory=*nike* (epinician)
praise to the thunder and to the weapon of
fire, the bolt that Zeus grasps in his   80
hand as master of storms—fit
emblem of triumphant
power in action! Our
elegant song will echo the
    pipe and its melodies,

5. coming at last from famed Dirka. When to a   Theban spring
father no longer young his   86
wife brings a much desired son
    he warms his mind with great
love, for wealth that must fall to the
care of an alien shepherd is to a
mortal a bitterly hateful thing.   90

So it is too, o Hagesidamos, when without
song a man of brave deeds goes to Hades,
breath spent for naught, toils wasted on
    joy all too brief! But upon
you, the soft-spoken lyre and the pipe now shed
joy, while Pierian maids, fathered by   95
Zeus, cherish your wide-spreading fame!

ep. I have zealously joined in their task,
embracing the glorious people of Lokris and

drenching their city of brave men in honey.
　　I praise Archestratos' handsome
son—I watched when the strength of his powerful fists　　　　100
triumphed beside the Olympian
shrine, fair himself and touched by the same
fullness of youth that
once (with aid from the Kyprian
goddess) kept Ganymede　　　　　　　　　　　　　　　105
　　safe from rude death.

OLYMPIAN 11   The Fox and the Lion

Like Olympian 10, for Hagesidamos of Western Lokris, son of Arch-
estratos and victor in the boxing ring.
476 BC

1. A time comes when winds are most needed by men,
another when rains from heaven are best,
offspring of storm-filled clouds, but
when after toil a man finds success, hymns sweetly sung can
lay the foundation of future renown—   5
pledged proof of glorious deeds!

Ungrudging praise is stored up for those victories
won at Olympia and, though the flower of
song-worthy thought comes only from god,
my tongue is eager to shepherd such words. Hagesidamos,   10
child of Archestratos, think upon this!
Thanks to your skill in the ring,

ep. I shall now crown your garland of olive and
gold by singing a sweet song of praise for the
men of Zephyrian Lokris. Join in their   15
revels, o Muses—I promise a visit,
not to a mob that shuns strangers and
scoffs at fine deeds, but to men skilled as
warriors who scale wisdom's peak!   19
      Neither the fox nor the bellowing
lion may alter the traits he was born with.   traits=cleverness/boldness

OLYMPIAN 12   An Exile's Good Fortune

For Ergoteles, a Cretan exile living in Himera, a city on the north shore of
Sicily, victor in the diaulos or long foot race of about four miles. Accord-
ing to a statue dedicated at Olympia, Ergoteles had two victories there
and others at Delphi, Nemea, and the Isthmos (Pausanias 6.4.11). Men of
Crete did not often compete at the great games, but many Sicilian ath-
letes did.

The opening reference to Zeus Eleutherios (giver of freedom, line 2)
is a reminder of the great victory over the invading Carthaginians won at
this place in 480 BC by combined forces from Syracuse and Akragas; it
may also refer to the overthrow, in 472 BC, of a very unpopular tyrant,
the son of Theron of Akragas.
470 or 466 BC

1. I beg you—o saving Chance, daughter of   Tyche
Zeus who gives freedom—to serve mighty Himera!   Zeus Eleutherios
You plot the course of swift ships at sea, of
unsteady battles on shore, and of those
civic assemblies where plans are devised.   5
Men's hopes ever surge high, then
sink as they journey through waves of illusion.

No earthling ever received from the gods a sure
signal, telling him what was to come. Men
look to the future with unseeing wits while
much that defies expectation appears—   10
joys are reversed but those who encounter
wind-blasts of pain may in an
instant trade grief for deep blessedness!

ep. Son of Philanor, your fame as a runner would
surely have wilted away like
that of a cock in his own barnyard had   15

faction not stolen your Knossian heritage.
Now, crowned once at Olympia, two times at
Pytho and twice at the Isthmos, o Ergoteles,
you bring renown to the nymphs' warm baths   Himera's hotsprings
   as you walk about in your fields!

For Xenophon of Korinth, son of Thessalos (likewise an athlete, lines 35–40), of the Oligathid tribe, victor in both stadium race (200 yards) and pentathlon (running, jumping, discus throw, javelin throw, wrestling). Xenophon had already won at Isthmia and Nemea, and his family could claim an enormous number of earlier victories (lines 34–46).

Pegasos was born from the throat of Medusa when Peleus took off her head (lines 63–4, cf. Pythian 10 and 12).

464 BC

1. Three times Olympian victor is the
house that I sing, gentle to townsmen,
helpful to strangers, and while I praise it I
come to know Korinth, gate to Poseidon's
Isthmian fields and city of glorious youth!   5
Here Eunomia dwells with her sisters,   civic order
   Dika, foundation of cities, and   justice
Peace, the protector of mortal wealth—
   three golden daughters of
Themis the counselor, all of them   cosmic order; cf. I. 8.31 ff.

ready to guard against Hybris, the   active insolence
quarrelsome mother of Koros. With   satisfied greed
fine deeds to tell, a confident boldness   11
urges my tongue to speak out. Character inborn
cannot be hidden. To you, o sons of Aletes,   legendary ruler of Korinth
when your bold deeds prevailed in the games that are
   sacred, the flower-decked Horai
often brought triumphant splendor—the   goddesses of youth
   same who cast so many
schemes for ancient devices   16

ep. into the hearts of your fellows!
    Everything has its inventor—
whence came the ox-driving dithyramb,
whence Dionysos' rejoicings? Who added
bridle to horses' tack, who placed twinned   20
bird-kings atop the gods' temples? In
Korinth the sweet-breathing Muse thrives,
here Ares flowers in youth's deadly spears!

2. Lord of Olympus, broad-ruling
king of the skies, father Zeus, let me   25
never offend with my words! I beg that,
keeping this people well beyond harm, you may
govern the windblast of Xenophon's fate.
Welcome this rite of crown-bearing revelry,
    dancers he leads back from Pisa
where he was pentathlon victor and   30
    first in the stadium race.
No one has ever surpassed him!

Two wreaths of celery covered his
brow at the Isthmian games, nor did
Nemea differ. His own sire, Thessalos,
offered the fame of his feet on Alpheos'   35
banks, and while the sun rose and set he
captured two prizes at Delphi, diaulos and
    stadium; in the same month,
at crag-bound Athens, one swift-footed
    day placed three superb
crowns in his curls—like to the seven

ep. taken in games here at Korinth.   40
    Lengthier songs will follow the
Isthmian exploits performed for
Poseidon by Terpsios and Eritimos,   cousins?
with Ptoiodoros their father. Your house has
taken how many garlands at Delphi

and in the Lion's Field? I face a multitude—   Nemea
I cannot number the sands of the sea!   46

3. Measure belongs to all things—to
know it brings best opportunity.
Sailing alone though part of this fleet,
I sing of past generations, praising their   50
wit and their brave deeds in battle, but telling no
lies about Korinth. I shall name Sisyphos,   legendary Korinthian king
    wily and shrewd as a god—
Medea too, who outfaced her
    father, married, and
rescued the Argo, both ship and crew.   cf. P. 4

And I shall tell of past bravery—how   55
both sides at Troy saw the issue of
battle as shaped by Korinthian courage,
those who as friends of the Atreids sought to
win Helen back, and those who meant to resist
at any cost. Greeks trembled when   60
    Glaukos came up out of Lykia,
boasting of ancestral rule, broad
    lands, and a palace in
Peirenē's city, derived from that   Korinth

ep. father who once at the nymph's spring   father=Bellerophon / nymph=Peirenē
    tried to tame Pegasos, child of the
snaky-haired Gorgon. He suffered much until
Pallas the virgin stepped from his dream as reality,   65
holding a bridle of gold, and spoke out:
"Do you sleep, o Aiolid king? Take this
horse-charm, offer a white bull to
father Damaios and show this to him!"   Poseidon, horse tamer

4. As he lay sleeping in shadow it   70
seemed that the Maid of the dark shield
uttered such words. He leapt to his feet and
finding the marvel that lay on the ground by his side, he

joyfully sought out the seer, the son of Koiranos, to
tell the whole tale—how by that prophet's own   75
   counsel he had for a night
slept at the goddess' altar, how
   she, the daughter of
Zeus of the thunderbolt spear, had herself

brought him a curb made of gold for his
steed. He was ordered to honor the
vision, and when a heavy-hoofed bull had been   80
slain for the Maker of Earthquakes, to
raise up an altar for Hippic Athena. Divine
power means easy completion even of
   deeds beyond hope or sworn oath.
So strong Bellerophon hastened to
   fix that gentling
charm 'round the jaw of the   85

ep. wing-borne horse; then he mounted and,
   bronze-clad, made play with his weapons.
Riding that steed, he sent arrows
down from chill pockets of air, to bring death to the
female Amazon horde, to Chimaira the
fire-breather, and to the Solymoi. His fate I   warlike tribe of Asia Minor
smother in silence; as for his mount—   91
he claims a stall in Olympian stables!

5. But, using two hands as I do, I must
not overshoot, casting my whirled spears
far past the target! I come in good   95
will as an ally of bright-throned Muses and Oligathids.
Manifold deeds done at Isthmia and too at
Nemea I shall depict with few
   words, for the sweet-sounding
shout of the herald, heard in those
   places a full sixty times,
serves as their witness, oath-bound.   100

Already told are their deeds at
Olympia; those yet to come I shall
sing in due time. All ends are wrought by the
gods, and my hopes are high: if familial fate
holds, we may leave their fulfillment with   105
Ares and Zeus. Six crowns were taken
   under the brow of Parnassos,
many at Argos and Thebes, and the royal
   shrine of the Lykaian
god has seen many more, as have

ep. Sikyon, Pellana, Megara, and too the
   well-fenced grove of the Aiakids,   on Aigina
Eleusis and rich Marathon, the wealthy   110
cities that lie beneath Aitna's high peak, and
those in Euboia! Search all Hellas—their victory
sites are too many to see! Come, and with light feet
swim back to shore. O Zeus of fulfillment, grant
awe with this portion of pleasure!   115

OLYMPIAN 14 The Graces

For Asopichos of Orchomenos, in Boiotia, son of Kleodamos (now dead, lines 20–21); winner in the boys' stadium race of 200 yards. 488 BC?

1. O Graces, famed for your song—you who take as your
portion a place where fine horses roam
close by the streams of Kephisos, you who are
queens of wealthy Orchomenos, patrons of Minyans of old—
listen to me as I pray! All things joyful and sweet   5
move among mortals in your company,
be a man fair, a fine singer, or of great fame. Never do
even the gods appoint dancing or feasts apart from the
much-revered Graces! Stewards of all heaven's deeds,
    they sit enthroned
close to the Pythian Apollo whose bow is of   10
gold, and they honor the power that flows
ceaselessly from the Olympian father.

2. Lady Aglaia and song-loving Euphrosyna,   cf. Hesiod *Theog.* 907–9
born to the strongest of gods, with Thalia
melody-mad, hear me and watch as this   15
congress of dancers skips high to mark our good fortune. My
care, as I come, is to sing of Asopichos, using the
Lydian mode, for thanks to you
this Minyan land can claim victory won at Olympia.
Go, Echo, now, down to the dark-walled   20
house of Persephonē! Take the true word of his
    fame to his father,
find Kleodamos and tell of the son who in
Pisa's famed valley has fixed in his hair
wings that were won in crown contest.   wings=wreaths, cf. P. 9.125

For Hieron of Syracuse (see Olympian 1 and Pythians 2 and 3), to cele-
brate a chariot victory taken at Delphi in 470 BC, and also to mark the
coronation, in that year, of Hieron's son, Deinomenes (named for his
grandfather), as king of the newly founded city of Aitna (lines 58 ff., cf.
the advice to the new ruler at lines 81–93). Hieron is suffering from ill
health (cf. Pythian 3) and is compared to Philoktetes, the lamed hero who
had to be brought to Troy by Greek warriors before that city could be
taken (lines 50–55).

   The latent force of the Sicilian volcano, which had erupted in 479 BC,
is employed as an emblem of chaos subdued by cosmic order, and this al-
lows the city founder, Hieron, to be presented as a mortal ruler who con-
tinues the work of Zeus within a tradition identified as Doric (lines 61–6).
470 BC

1. Lyre made of gold, you speak for Apollo
and for the dark-haired Muses! Dancing feet,
    splendor's beginning, obey you and
voices respond to your signal when
vibrating strings sound the opening notes that
    lead out the chorus.
You can extinguish the warlike bolt of   5
immortal fire and bring sleep to the eagle
    poised on the sceptre of Zeus,
    swift wings drooping at either side—

king of the birds! Over his head and his
bent neck you pour a darkening cloud, a sweet
    closing of eyes, and he rests,
rippling his liquid back, conquered by
your tides of sound. Fierce Ares forgets his sharp   10
    spear, his heart warmed by
slumber, for your shafts of music take

even the wits of the gods in their spell when
    aimed with the skill of Apollo
    and of the deep-bosomed Muses!

ep. But all those that Zeus does not love are
stricken with fear by the voice of the
    maids of Pieria, whether on land   Muses
or in the alien sea—even he who lies in dread   15
Tartaros, Typhon the hundred-head foe of the gods   Hesiod *Theog.* 820 ff.
reared in the fabled Kilikian cave.
Now sea-washed heights beyond Kymē, Sicily too,
weigh on his shaggy-haired chest, while snowy
    Aitna, pillar of heaven and
nurse of perpetual snow, pins him down.   20

2. Fountains of pure unapproachable fire are
belched from within; rivers of kindling smoke
    pour forth by day while at night
churning red flames send boulders rumbling
down to the depths of the sea with a crash. That
    monster spits out
torrents that blaze with Hephaistos' most terrible   25
power, a portent dreadful to
    see, dreadful even to
    hear of from those who have watched.

Such is he who lies chained under Aitna's dark
tree-covered heights and its plain, his couch
    sharp as a goad to his outstretched back!
May we, o Zeus, ever be pleasing to
you who govern this peak, brow of a   30
    fruit-bearing land where a
glorious founder gives to the neighboring
city the same name—"Aitna"—pro-
    claimed by the herald who
    cried out the news of Hieron's

ep. chariot crown! For sailors just
launched on a voyage a favoring
      wind is a blessed gift, an omen of
happy return. By this rule our good fortune today   35
brings expectations of garlands to come, of prize-winning
horses and fame to be gained for this city at
musical festivals. O Phoibos, Lykian   Apollo
ruler of Delos, friend to Parnassos and
      Kastalia's spring, may it please you to
make this a country of valiant men!   40

3. Gods grant the means to mortal success, while
nature makes poets, fine speakers and men of strength.
      Eager am I to give praise,
but I would not, like an athlete,
brandish my bronze-tipped spear and then cast it
      outside the mark—I
hope for a throw that excels over others. Let   45
oncoming Time hold his wealth and his happiness   his=Hieron's
      to a straight course!
      May he forget all his toil while

yet he remembers the wartime battles—
how he stood with bold heart, and with god-given
      skills reaped such honors as no other
Hellene has known, crowning his wealth.
Like Philoktetes, he went to war when a   50
      proud friend, hard-pressed,
crawled at his feet. God-like heroes, they say,
crossed over to Lemnos to bring
      that son of Poias to Troy,
      though he was nagged by his wound.

ep. He was the one who as an archer
brought Priam's city to ruin and
      finished the task of the Greeks, walking on
weak legs but carrying fate! May some god work a   55
like revival for Hieron, opening chances for

all he desires! Muse, I ask that you
stand with Deinomenes, singing the ransom that's
owed for this team of four horses. His father's
   victory joy is not foreign to him—let's
fashion a song now, for Aitna's king!   60

4. His is the city that Hieron built with
god-sponsored freedom, according to Hyllos' set   son of Herakles
   rule. Descendants of Herakles
and of Pamphylos who dwell on the
slopes of Taÿgetos choose ever to honor the   above Sparta
   laws of Aigimios as   legendary Doric lawgiver
Dorians. Come down from Pindos, this blessed   65
tribe took Amyklai and there, as friends of the   cf. I. 7.14–5
   Tyndarid lords of white horses, the   Kastor and Pollux
   fame of their lances yet blooms.

Zeus of fulfillment, grant to the townsmen and
kings who dwell by the streams of Amenas a   river near Aitna
   like fate, told as enduring truth!
Aided by you, their leader may honor his
people and turn them toward song-filled tranquility,   70
   teaching his son
by his example. Grant, son of Kronos, that
howling Etruscans keep mildly at home, Cartha-
   ginians too—their rage at Kymē
   brought grief to their own fleet, and,   474 BC

ep. tamed by the ruler of Syracuse, they
watched as their youth were cast into the
   sea from the decks of their ships while he
rescued all Greece from slavery's burden. At   75
Athens I gain thanks with songs about Salamis,
at Sparta by singing the Kithairon battle where   Platea, 479 BC
Medes bent their bows and then suffered, but here on
Himera's sea-washed coast I sound out the hymn
   owed to Deinomenes' sons for the courage   Gelo and Hieron
they spent to weary that enemy host.   Battle of Himera, 480 BC

5. Speak to the moment, into a short length twist   advice for singers / rulers
multiple ends and less blame will follow.
    Surfeit may blunt the sharp edge of
hope, while talk of fine deeds not their
own leaves townspeople heavy at heart, but—since
    envy is better than
pity—never shun noble attempts!   85
Govern, taking your post at the
    rudder of justice, your tongue
    shaped on the anvil of truth!

Coming from you, guardian of many, the
least flying spark will seem great and many will
    testify, for and against.
If you would gain sweet repute you must
keep a fair temper and never grow   90
    tired of expense.
Let out your sail to the wind like a
helmsman, my friend, but do not be tricked by
    dubious gains. Only the
    fame that comes after, sounded in

ep. story and song, will reveal how
earlier men ordered their lives.
    Kroisos' kind deeds do not wither but everywhere
tales filled with hatred fix upon Phalaris, whose bronze   95
bull roasted men. His name finds no   tyrant of Akragas, ca. 550 BC
welcome at feasts, nor do lyres and the whispering
voices of boys make him their sweet common
theme! A man strives for prosperity, then for renown;
    he who meets both—and takes hold—
wins for himself the highest of crowns.   100

PYTHIAN 2   The Rape of a Cloud

Again for Hieron, ruler of Syracuse and chariot victor, but the circumstances are unknown. Nothing in the ode indicates a particular festival or year, though the reference to Lokris (line 19) means that its composition must have come later than 476 BC, the year of Hieron's first intervention in south Italy.

Evidently, the court has been disturbed by dissidents who slander the ruler (lines 75–81) and favor a nameless rival (the "ape" of line 72), but this ode, in contrast to the negative sordidness of iambic blame (line 55), calls itself a battle song transformed to become a hymn of praise (lines 69–70). The singers end with an affirmation of loyalty to the order that Hieron has established, while urging him to live up to their ideal portrait of him (lines 71–2).

Ixion killed his father-in-law (lines 31–2) but was pardoned by Zeus and received among the gods as their guest; as punishment for his subsequent attempt upon Hera (lines 33–4), he was fastened to a wheel that whirled forever through space (line 40).

Post 476 BC

1. Syracuse—strongest of cities, precinct of
Ares Lord of War's Depths, god-chosen trainer of
    panoplied horses and men—I
come from rich Thebes, bringing you song! Here's
news of an earthshaking four-horse
car that gives triumph to Hieron, keeper of   5
chariots! Ortygia, where Artemis dwells,   cf. N. 1.1–2; O. 6.92
he wreathes in far-shining crowns, for only with
help from the fluvial goddess did his gentle hands
    master those fancy-reined fillies!

She, divine archer and virgin, aided by
Hermes, master of games, settles his team in its
    glittering harness with her two hands

67

each time he fastens their strength to his
well-polished chariot, summoning
aid from the wide-ruling god of the
trident. For other kings, others make   Poseidon, god of horses
far-sounding hymns—so Kyprian men   15
often sing Kinyras, much loved by   cf. Homer *Il.* 11.20 ff.
    gold-tressed Apollo, and

ep. priest and favorite of Aphrodite. Gratitude,
    rendered with awe, comes in return for a
man's friendly deeds. O son of Deinomenes,
you are hailed by the maid of Zephyrian Lokris—
    eyes free of fear she
stands at her doorstep, saved by your strength from   20
war's devastation! Whirling on high,
fixed by the will of the gods to his winged
wheel, Ixion announces this rule for mankind: The
giver of bounty must be well repaid with
    frequent and warm compensation.

2. That much he learned. As friend of the Kronian   25
gods, he shared their sweet life but could not
    endure such great bliss; wits astray, he
dared to love Hera whose place was in Zeus'
pleasure-filled couch! Arrogance
urged him to insolent madness and soon he
had as his due a pain like no other, determined   30
by his two crimes—he had been first to stain men with
kin-blood (nor did he act without plan),
    and he had entered the echoing

marriage-hall meaning to ravish the bed-mate of
Zeus. Always a mortal must measure by his own
    stature. Unsanctioned coupling
plunges the culprit into a chaos of   35
evil and such was his fate when—
ignorant creature!—he chased a sweet lie and
lay with a cloud. She seemed the daughter of

Kronos, but what he took was a trick, a beautiful bane of
Zeus' invention. So he wrought for himself a   40
   four-spoked wheel of destruction, a

ep. prison from which, inescapably fettered, he
   cries out his message to all.   message, cf. line 24
She, the illusion, bore him, apart from the Graces, one
overbold child as strange as herself, who knew no
   honor, either on
earth or in heaven. She called him Kentauros,   "one who rapes the air"
reared him, and he later mixed with Magnesian   45
mares in the foothills of Pelion, to sire a most
marvelous herd that resembled both parents—
like to their mothers below but above, in
   torso and head, like the father.

3. God ever reaches the goal he intends—
god who can capture the eagle in flight,   50
   swim past the dolphin at sea, or
bring down the arrogant man while granting to
others an unchanging glory. But
I must ever avoid the sharp bite of calumny.
I've seen the distant Archilochos,   poet of the 7th c. BC
master of blame, grown fat upon words stuffed with   55
hatred, but helpless. Wealth got by a fate-filled
   chance is wisdom's best aim, and

this you possess to display with free heart as   you=Hieron
guardian and lord of these fortified streets
   and of your army. If anyone
names some long-ago Hellene as higher in
honor or riches, he picks a fool's fight!   60
I shall embark on a ship wreathed in flowers,
singing of splendid deeds. Boldness
shown in fierce battles accords well with
youth and this I announce as the source of the
   limitless fame you have found,

ep. striving among mounted men or those on foot.   65
    Now your good counsels, more
ripe than your years, bring to each part of my laud
claims unassailable. May you fare well! This
    music is sent, like
cargo from Carthage, over the silvery
sea—receive it with favor, a Kastor-song   Spartan battle song
set to Aiolian chords, gift of the seven-stringed lyre!   70
Hearing this praise, learn who you are and
strive to become that same one! Among children an
    ape is ever found fair—yes, fair!

4. but Rhadamanthys' good fortune endures   cf. O. 2.76
thanks to the blameless fruit of his mind, nor does he
    secretly savor those sly whispered
lies that track a man down. Speakers of   75
slander, foxes in temper,
cause strong evil to both sides so how does such
wiliness profit them? Like that of tackle,
their work is done in the depths of the sea, while
I move above, untouched by the brine, the   80
    cork that floats over the net.

Speaking to those who are noble, the devious
citizen has no effect; he fawns upon all and
    weaves his own ruin. I want no
part of his impudence! I would be friend to my
friend but as enemy, wolf-like, I'd
track down my foe, sometimes taking a sinuous   85
path. Each polity values the man who speaks
truth, be it ruled by tyrant or turbulent mob—
even where wise men watch over the city!
    No man should strive with a god who

ep. now favors these, then brings fame at its highest to
    others, but envious
minds are not soothed by this truth. Excessively   90

eager, they strain at the starting-cord, driving a
    painful wound into their
hearts, their ambitions never attained.
Better by far to take the yoke lightly
onto one's back and bear it. Kick at the
goad and you'll end on a slippery path.   95
O let me gratify those who are noble,
    ever enjoying their company!

For Hieron of Syracuse. Neither occasion nor date is known, though Pythian victories taken by the race-horse Pherenikos (who won at Olympia in 476 BC, cf. Olympian 1) are mentioned (lines 73–4). Because the poet's "voice" sounds more clearly here than in any other ode, many scholars call this a "poetic epistle," but its form shows that a choral performance was expected. The song belongs to the period in which the foundation of Aitna (cf. Pythian 1) was either in progress or recently completed (line 69), and it is usually assigned to 474 BC.
474 BC

1. I wish—if the plea of all men may
come from my tongue—that,
   though he is dead,
Chiron, the son of Philyra and of Ouranian   cf. P. 4.102, 115; 9.29; N. 3.53; 4.60;
Kronos, lived yet and ruled in Pelion's   I. 8.41
   glens as a wilderness creature
friendly to man, just as he was when he   5
bred up Asklepios, maker of
   strengthening cures and
hero-protector from every disease!

Phlegyas' daughter, before she could   Koronis
bring him to birth with
   help from the goddess, was   Eleithyia, cf. N. 7.1; O. 6.42
mastered by Artemis' arrow of gold; from her   10
chamber she went, by Apollo's design, down to
   Hades. The children of Zeus are not
light in their anger but she, like a fool, paid no
mind, hid from her father and promised her
   couch to a stranger, when
already mated with long-haired Apollo and

ep. carrying his divine seed. Nor would she wait,   15
either for marriage-feast or for the
many-voiced gibes that
friends still unwed love to shout at a
bride from their twilight convoys of song.
She yearned for faraway things, as many do—   20
one tribe of men, the vainest of all, scorns
what lies at hand to stare into the distance,
chasing futility with empty hopes.

2. Such dread delusion belonged to the
will of Koronis,   25
     couched by a
passing Arkadian! Nor was her deed without witness.
Far off at Pytho, where sheep bleed, the shrine's lord,
     Loxias, learned of it, told by that   Apollo
best of advisors, his all-seeing mind.
Lies touch him not, nor can he be
     cheated by act or by
scheme, whether of god or of man.   30

He knew of her impious trick, the
guest-bed prepared for
     Ischyos, Elatos'
son, and he sent his own sister, raging with terrible   Artemis, line 10
power, to Boibias' shore where the girl dwelt.   Lakereia, in Thessaly
Then her fate shifted, bringing harsh
ruin upon her, and many a neighbor   35
perished as well. So, in the mountains,
     flame from one spark may
spread to consume all the trees in a forest.

ep. But when kinsmen had placed the girl inside a
pyre-wall and hungry flames ran all around,
Apollo spoke out: 40
"I cannot bear to destroy my own
     son in piteous death as part of his
mother's sore grief!" He took a stride and, as the

blazing fire parted, snatched out the babe from the
corpse and carried him off to the centaur to   Chiron
study the healing of man's painful ills.

3. Those who came suffering from home-grown
sores, those whose limbs were
   pierced by bronze blades or
broken by far-flying stones, others with flesh ravaged by
sunstroke or winter's sharp cold—these he   50
   freed from their ills. Some were
healed with soft chants, some with potions that
soothed or with herbs to be bound upon
   wounds, while others yet were
set on their feet with the cut of his knife.

But gain may trap science itself. Gold,
placed in his palm, bought   55
   even this hero, a
princely wage offered for bringing a man back from death.
Zeus tore the breath from the pair, fiery   Asklepios/the revived
   doom in the bolt that his two hands
cast. We must seek from the gods
only what's scaled to our own mortal
   wits—eyes fixed on the
path just ahead, aware of our fate.   60

ep. Ask not, o my soul, for a life without death
but, of the possible, take the last
drop! If wise Chiron were
still in his cave and if hymns could
charm him with sweetness, I would have begged that he   65
once again send among mortals a healer of
their fevered ills, some son of Apollo or Zeus.
Then I'd have crossed the Ionian Sea to
reach Arethusa's pure spring, where my Aitnaian   cf. N. 1.1–3

4. host rules as king over Syracuse,   host=Hieron
gentle with citizens,
                                                                71

open with nobles, a
father to guests! Had I arrived with two gifts—
good health and dancers to glorify crowns from the
    Pythian games, taken at Kirrha   in 482 BC and 478 BC
by Pherenikos—the deep sea once passed
I might have risen for him as a   75
    rescuing light, shining
further than any bright star in the sky!

Still, I shall send up a prayer to that
Mother so often   Magna Mater=Rhea/Kybele
    sung at my gate with
Pan (at evening by troupes of young girls)—
goddess most holy! If, Hieron, you have taken the   80
    point of old sayings, you know that the
gods choose to send, for each happy gift,
two that bring pain. Fools do not bear this truth
    quietly but with its
fair side turned outward the best men do.

ep. You are pursued by a fortunate fate—
destiny favors the ruler who   85
cares for his people.
Life without risk came neither to
Peleus, Aiakos' son, nor to
Kadmos, yet both reached the summit of bliss when
crowned Muses sang—on Pelion's peak or at   90
Thebes—as the one wed Harmonia, the other famed
Thetis, wise Nereus' daughter.   cf. N. 4.65–8; N. 5.22.4

5. Gods dined with both and the two men
looked on the royal
    children of Kronos,
seated on golden thrones; they received gifts and   95
with ancient sorrows reversed, thanks to Zeus,
    both hearts revived. True, the sufferings
of his three daughters soon robbed Kadmos of   Ino, Autonoe, Agave
joy, but father Zeus did afterward

take his desire to the sweet
couch of the fourth, the white-armed Thyonē!   Semele, mother of Dionysos

As for the one child of Peleus,   Achilles
born in Phthia to   101
    immortal Thetis,
he died, struck by an arrow in battle, and loud lament
came from the Danaan host at his pyre. A
    mortal whose mind takes the pathway of
truth must rejoice in what the gods send.
Gusts of high wind blow helter-skelter and   105
    striking with force, man's bliss
neither stays whole nor rests long.

ep. I shall be low when my fortunes are low,
grand among grandeurs, giving such
care as I can to the
lot I receive. If soft wealth should   110
come from a god I shall hope for eventual
glory. Sarpedon and Nestor stay in men's speech
thanks to the echoing verses that poets have
fitted to them. Prowess endures in praises well
sung, but few find these easy to earn!   115

For Arkesilas IV, hereditary king of Cyrene (Kyrana), a rich city on the North African coast, to celebrate the victory of his chariot, which was driven by his brother-in-law, Karrhotos. Cyrene was founded ca. 630 BC by settlers from the island of Thera (Santorini) and was still ruled by the descendants of their leader, Battos (lines 5, 52, 68, 280), though the nobility had at times been rebellious. The Damophilos who dominates the close of the ode (lines 282 ff.) was an exile whom the king seems to have decided to recall in a gesture meant to defuse aristocratic discontent.

The mythic section (lines 68–246) treats the tale of the Argonauts, showing Jason as a young hero who, like an athlete, undertakes a severe trial and with divine aid wins a crown in a set contest (line 240). This account, however, is prefaced by a later episode from the Argo's return journey, in which Medea's voice (lines 12–56) concentrates attention not on the Golden Fleece that Jason brings back to Iolkos but instead on an ominous clod of earth that has been lost, although it controls the eventual foundation of Cyrene by Battos. Medea explains that while chance can interrupt destiny, its effects can only be temporary—a useful thought when a royal policy is to be reversed.

The Golden Fleece had belonged to a miraculous ram that flew to the rescue of a Theban prince, Phrixos, about to be sacrificed to Poseidon by his stepmother (lines 158–61). The ram then flew eastward to Kolchis, at the far end of the Black Sea, where Phrixos, having found safety with the local ruler, offered it in sacrifice and hung up its hide on a tree, where it was guarded by a dragon (lines 241–46).
462 BC

1. This day, o Muse, you must stand with a friend, the
ruler of horse-loving Kyrana! Revel with
    Arkesilas! Encourage this fair wind of song
owed to the offspring of Leto and also to Pytho
    where, long ago, she who
sits with the golden eagles of Zeus   the Delphic priestess

did, when Apollo was near, name Battos as   oracle given ca. 630 BC
chosen by god to be founder of rich Libya!   6
    Leaving the sacred isle,   isle=Thera
he was to build, on earth's luminous
breast, a city of chariot-drivers.

This, after seven and ten generations, would
satisfy words that the furious lady of   10
    Kolchis, Medea, the child of Aietes, had
long ago uttered at Thera—counsel from immortal
    lips for the hero-companions of
Jason the warrior. "Hear me," she cried, "you
sons of brave men and of gods! One day a
root from this sea-beaten isle will be nurtured by
    Epaphos' daughter and   daughter=Libya
cities beloved of men will   15
grow where Zeus Ammon is heard!   an oracular site in Libya

ep. Men of this place will trade winged dolphins for   for this place=Thera
    swift racing horses and
change oars for reins to guide chariots fast as the
    wind. That token of powerful
cities to come will yet be fulfilled with
Thera as mother—omen received months ago at the   20
    mouth of Lake Triton when, in the
form of a man, a god proffered earth as a
guest-gift and hero Euphamos leapt
down from the ship to receive it. Kronian
    Zeus marked the moment with

2. favoring thunder, sent just as we hauled up our
bronze-fitted anchor, swift Argo's bridle. Twelve   25
    days we had carried our seagoing bark over
desolate dry land, following my advice, when
    suddenly that lone god
made his appearance, wearing the bright
confident face of a gracious and reverent
man. He accosted us, using the language of

friendship, such as a
generous host may employ when   30
calling his guests to a banquet, but

we urged our need for a sweet return home.
He gave his name as Eurypylos, son of the
    Earthshaker Ennosidas, and seeing our   Poseidon
haste he scooped up some soil in his right hand—a
    happenstance guest-gift—and
offered it. Nor was the gesture refused, for the   35
hero, jumping ashore, took the fate-filled
earth from the palm of the stranger into his own.
    Now I am told that this
clod has been washed from the ship in the
evening spray, to follow the

ep. watery currents below! Many times I have   40
    urged the servants who
save us from toil to keep a close guard, but
    they have forgotten and so the
undying seed of broad Libya is poured out
too soon, and here on this isle! If, on return, he had
    cast it into the hell-mouth at
holy Mount Tainaros—he, Euphamos, the   in Lakedaimon
son of Poseidon and born on the   45
banks of Kephisos to Tityos' daughter,
    Europa—then would his

3. race, in its fourth generation, have gone out   in the 12th c. BC
with the Danaans to take that broad land, for
    many at that time will go forth from Sparta, the
gulf of the Argives, and from Mykenai. Now he must
    visit the couches of
alien women to found the race   on Lemnos, cf. line 253
chosen, with honor from god, to settle this   51
island where *he* must be born—he who will rule in those   he=Battos
    cloud-shadowed plains. In   Libya

time he will enter the treasure-filled
Pythian shrine and Phoibos with   cf. above lines 4–6

prophetic voice will command him to lead   55
shiploads of colonists down to the rich Nile
    precinct of Zeus." Thus did Medea
order her words and, stunned by her dense thought, the
    heroes fell silent.
O Polymnastos' most blessed son, your   son=Battos
part in this tale was confirmed by the unsought
voice of the priestess at Delphi when   60
    three times she hailed you as
"Kyrana's fore-destined King!"
though you had come only to

ep. ask the gods' price for release from your blighted
    speech. And so, even
now, as if at the rose-filled zenith of
    spring, in the eighth generation,
your line comes into bloom with Arkesilas,   65
to whom Apollo and Pythian judges give
    fame in the chariot race.
I here offer him up to the Muses,   cf. line 1
along with the Golden Fleece! When the
Minyans set out in pursuit of that prize, god-sent   people of northern Greece
    honors were planted for them, but

4. what was the cause—what danger bound them with   70
fetters of steel to this voyage? For Pelias,   ruler of Iolkos
    death was ordained, to come from an
Aiolid source, wrought by plots or by violence—   Aiolids=Jason's tribe
    such was the oracle
brought from the tree-shaded navel of earth. It
chilled his shrewd heart, telling him ever to
guard against him who would wear but one sandal, a   75
    man who would come from the
steep heights down to the sun-filled
plains of famed Iolkos, whether as

stranger or townsman. And one day he came—
fearsome, grasping two lances and clothed in two
   fashions, his marvellous limbs covered by
native Magnesian garb while the skin of a leopard
   shielded his head from
shivering rain. Nor were the locks of his
glorious hair cut short—they shadowed his
spine as he strode, swift and straight, into the
   crowd at the market to
take his stand there, daring to
put his unshakable purpose on trial.

80

85

ep. They knew him not, but stared while a voice
   spoke from the mob, "Can
this be Apollo—or Ares of the bronze
   chariot, husband of Kypris?
Iphimedeia's two sons are said to have
met death on Naxos—Otos and you, o valorous
   prince Epialtes! And surely the
arrow that Artemis took from her conquering
quiver struck Tityos down, teaching
men to seek only such loves as
   come within mortal reach?"

giants killed by Apollo

90

giant who tried to rape Leto

5. Into this murmuring crowd came Pelias,
driving his polished mule-cart with speed.
   Seeing the single conspicuous sandal
bound to the stranger's right foot, he was stunned but with
   fear hidden deep in his
heart he challenged him: "Stranger, what
place do you claim as your fatherland? Which of earth's
gutter-bred hags dropped you from her
   over-aged womb?
Name the race of your forebears and
do not defile them with odious lies!"

95

100

Boldly, though using mild words, the other
replied, "A pupil of Chiron's, I come from the

cave where Philyra and Chariklo, chaste   *mother and wife of Chiron*
daughters of Kentauros, cared for me. Through   *cf. P. 2.44–9*
   twenty years' time, no
unruly expression of mine
ever offended those friends. Now I come home,   105
claiming the throne of my father, unjustly
   stolen from him though long ago
granted by Zeus to lord Aiolos,   *cf. line 72*
leader of men, and to his race.

ep. I'm told that Pelias, true to his lawless and
   cowardly heart, has
taken these honors by force from right-ruling   110
   kinsmen of mine. Those men,
knowing that lord and his arrogant violence,
feared for me, and when I first saw the light,
   they mixed laments with women's shrill
cries, as if for a death, wrapped me in
purple swaddling clothes and,
   trusting the night, secretly sent me away to the   115
   care of the Kronian Chiron.

5. That is the gist of my tale. Now tell me plainly,
you worthy citizens, which is the house of my
   fathers, riders of white steeds? As son of
Aison and born here, I am no stranger among you. The
   gods' beast addressed me as   *beast=Chiron*
Jason." Such was his speech. As he entered the hall,
his father's eyes knew him at once and tears   120
burst from his ancient lids, though
   all through his soul he felt
joy as he looked on his exiled son,
come to him now as the fairest of men.

News of him spread and soon two uncles joined them—
Pheres appeared from the nearby Hyperian
   spring, Amythaon soon after out of Messenē;   125
then, with Melampos, Admetos arrived in all haste,

both moved by loyalty
owed to their cousin. Jason received them with
banquets and honey-sweet words, his
due hospitality heightened by mirth of all kinds.
    Through five full days and through
five nights they gathered the finest of
life's sacred joys; then on the   130

ep. sixth he began from the start, telling his
        kinsmen the whole of his
urgent intent. They agreed, and with him they
        leapt from their couches, rushed to the
great hall of Pelias, burst in and there took a
stand. Hearing their clamor, that lord   135
        (son of the lovely-haired Tyro)
came to confront them but Jason, gentle by
nature, established a basis for sense with a soft
voice, saying, "Son of Poseidon breaker of rocks,
        men's minds are ever too

7. quick to admire cunning profit rather than
justice, though all of us creep toward a bitter   140
        tomorrow, but you and I, to shape a rich
future, must govern our passions. This we both know:
        wild Salmoneus and   their great-grandfathers
Krethos were born to one mother and
we two look on the sun's golden force being
both of the same third generation. The
        Fates turn away when
enmity moves among kinsmen and   145
shame-bound Respect disappears.   Aidos

We are not meant to use lances or bronze-fitted
swords to divide our inherited honors.
    Sheep-flocks and herds of pale cattle I
give you and with them the fields that you stole from my
        fathers to fatten your
wealth—that your house now feeds upon these is   150

not my concern. But the scepter of royalty
and too the throne where Kretheus' son sat as he
   rendered straight judgments
among his brave knights—these
you must release, with pain neither

suffered nor given, lest some fresh evil should   155
   rise up between us!"
He spoke, and Pelias soothingly answered,
   "I shall behave as you ask but
age is already upon me while your youth only now
blooms—you might soften the rage of the dead!
   Phrixos commands us to
bring back his soul from Aietes' far chambers and
with it the thick woolly cloak of the   160
ram that saved him from drowning
   and from his stepmother's

8. impious weapons. A marvellous dream
told me of this and when I inquired at Kastalia,   Delphi
   asking if I should obey, the oracle
urged that a ship be readied at once and sent off.
   Finish this task, and
I undertake to resign both power and   165
crown! To this, my solemn oath, let Zeus be our
witness, ancestral god to us both!" They
   parted, well-pleased with their
pact, and Jason at once sent out
heralds proclaiming his imminent

voyage to all. First to respond were   170
three sons of Kronian Zeus, all tireless in   Kastor, Pollux, Herakles
   battle, born to Leda and bright-eyed Alkmena;
next came two others sired by the Earthshaker,   Poseidon
   hair knotted high and
proud of their courage, one out of Pylos, the
other from Tainaros' cliffs—Euphamos and
you, o strong Periklymenos!—whose noble
                                       175

glory would soon be secured.
And from Apollo came Orpheus,
father of lyre-song, while Hermes whose

ep. staff is of gold sent two of his sons to this
    long-lasting trial,
Echion and also Eurytos, both
    brimming with youth. Soon, from the
foot of Pangaion, another pair came,   180
Zetēs and Kalaïs, armed and dispatched with
    smiling good will by their father,
Boreas, king of the winds, each sporting
violet wings that stretched from his back.
Such was the sweet all-persuading desire for the
    Argo enkindled by

9. Hera in these demigods—not, left behind, to   185
savor a life led close to one's mother, but
    rather to go out with age-mates to
search for the magic of courage, and to discover it,
    though at the cost of death!
When these prize sailors had gathered at Iolkos
Jason reviewed them with praise; then Mopsos the
seer, when he had cast sacred lots and consulted the   190
    birds, in full gladness
sent all aboard with good augury.
Anchors once hung at the prow, the captain

stood at the stern, raising a golden cup, and called
first upon Zeus of the fire-bolt, then upon winds,
    swift-rolling waves, sea-roads easily
found in the night, favoring days, and a friendly   195
    homecoming fate. From the
clouds came an answering thunderclap,
spears of bright lightning splintered and fell, and the
heroes, trusting such signs from the god,
    took in fresh life with each

breath. The master of portents
voiced his fair expectations and,   200

ep. with the command that oars should be
   seized, a tireless rowing
sprang from their practiced hands. Breezes
   out of the south carried them up to the
mouth of the Unfriendly Sea and there, finding a   the Black Sea
full herd of red Thracian bulls and a
   new-made stone altar ready for
fire, they set up a shrine for the   205
sea-god Poseidon. About to be
swept toward a deep pit of danger, they
   prayed to the Shipmaster,

10. asking escape from the furious crush of the   cf. A.R. *Arg.* 2.549–610
Clashing Rocks for, rolling together, that living
   pair was faster than loud roaring winds
(though these voyaging heroes would finish their threat).   210
   Reaching the Phasis they   river at Kolchis
dropped sail and, watched by Aietes, did
battle with dark-featured Kolchian men. Then the
goddess whose arrows are sharpest fastened the   Aphrodite
   glittering iunx to a   the wryneck, a bird of erotic compulsion
four-spoked wheel that could
not be escaped and for the first time   215

brought that maddening bird from Olympus
down to dwell among men. She taught Jason
   prayers and chants to expel from the
heart of Medea all daughterly duty, leaving it
   goaded by Peitho and   erotic persuasion
fired with a longing for Greece, and the girl
showed him at once how to perform the   220
trials her father would set. She gave him a
   salve made of oil and
pain-killing herbs, and the two
promised to join in the sweet marriage act.

ep. Aietes then dragged out an iron plough and
    to it led oxen who
breathed out live fire from pale jaws and in turn   225
    tore at the ground with their brazen
hooves. Single-handed he yoked them and
drove them straight on, cutting furrows as
    deep as six feet in the
earth's muddy back. Then he spoke, "When your
king—or whoever that is who governs your
ship—has completed this tillage,   230
    he may at once take the

10. unchanging hide—the Fleece fringed with gold!"
Jason in answer threw off his saffron-dyed
    cloak and laid hands to his work, trusting in god.
Balked by words from the mistress of magic, the   Medea
    fire could not touch him; he
pulled the plough to him, fatally bound both
beasts by the neck and, thrusting his pitiless   235
goad deep into their ribs, accomplished by force the
    length that was set.
Aietes, agape at the strength shown,
howled with unspeakable pain, but

Jason's companions stretched out their hands,
piled grassy crowns on his head, and hailed him with   240
    honey-sweet words. Then Helios' crafty son   Aietes
told them of Phrixos' sacred knives—what they had
    wrought and where the bright fleece had been
hung, for he still believed that the trial to
come would be more than his foe could achieve—the
hide was now deep in a forest, clenched in the
    jaws of a dragon more
huge and more swift than a fifty-oared   245
ship crafted by men's iron tools.

ep. But travel by highroad is long. Time presses and
    I know a shortcut

where other singers may follow! That
   silver-eyed scaly-backed monster
he killed by cunning, o Arkesilas, and   250
then stole a willing Medea—for Pelias an
   agent of death—touched Okeanos' broad
streams and the Red Sea and came at last to the
land of the man-killing Lemnian wives.   cf. line 50
There for the prize of a cloak they
   tested the strength of their   for these games, cf. O. 4.20–3

11. limbs, then bedded the women. In those   255
alien fields, one fateful day (perhaps night) took the
   seed of your family's fortunes, and thus
planted the line of Euphamos continues
   forever. In due time your
forebears, passing from Sparta, settled the
isle of Kallista, whence they set out when   Thera, cf. line 52
Leto's fair son gave to your race, with honors from   above, lines 3–8; 58–63
   Heaven, the care of the
Libyan plain and the city of
gold-throned Kyrana, where you yet   260

govern, devising right counsel. Think on the
wisdom of Oidipous! Should a man take up an
   axe to chop off the limbs of a splendid
oak he will ruin a beautiful form but the trunk, though
   barren, will testify
still to its nature, whether it comes in the   265
end to a winter's hearth-fire, or at last
serves among lordly roof-pillars, giving its
   painful support to
alien walls while its faraway
home is stripped and deprived.

ep. You are a most timely healer—your light is   270
   honored by Paian!   Apollo as healer
Best treat a festering wound with a
   light hand; easy it is, even for

powerless men, to shatter a city, but
difficult ever to settle it back in its place
    unless some god should come
suddenly down to govern its rulers!
And yet such blessings unfold for you as a   275
finished web! Dare, then, to spend your full
    zeal on Kyrana!

12. Ponder the counsel of Homer and heed it: "In
every affair," so he said, "a good messenger
    brings highest honor." Even the Muse gains
grandeur from words truly spoken. The palace of
    Battos—indeed
all of Kyrana!—knows the just temper of   280
Damophilos. Young among youths but in counsel a
hundred years old, he robs the slandering
    tongue of its rancorous
voice and has learned to despise the
author of arrogant deeds while

holding no quarrel with men who are noble—   285
nor is he slow to achieve. Opportunity
    makes short visits to men but he knows it
well and keeps near, its servant but never its drudge. The
    worst of all griefs is to
glimpse a fair deed that can't be approached.
This man, distanced like Atlas from
home and possessions, has wrestled with
heaven, but immortal Zeus did once   290
    loosen the bonds of the
Titans, and after a time, as the wind changes,
sails come to be shifted. With his

ep. cup of misfortune now drained, he
    prays he may someday see
home once again—may join those who
    drink at the well of Apollo,
giving his heart to the pleasures of youth,   295

or may in quietude take up his elegant lyre among
    citizen singers, offering
pain to no man, himself without grief.
Then, o Arkesilas, he might tell of the
wellspring of undying words, found when
    Thebes made him welcome!

PYTHIAN 5 Battos and the Founding of Cyrene

Again for Arkesilas, king of Cyrene (Kyrana), in celebration of the same
victory as that of Pythian 4. This time, however, the ode is meant for pub-
lic performance at the Lakonian Karneia (line 80), a citywide musical fes-
tival that marked the culture of Cyrene as Doric (lines 72–82). Featuring
a dance of young men in armor, it emphasized the military function of
the Battiad aristocracy. For the tale of Battos and the city's foundation,
see Pythian 4.
462 BC

1. Wealth has broad strength when,
mixed with clean prowess and offered by
fate, it comes to a mortal who knows it as
bringer of friends!
This you have sought, o god-portioned   5
Arkesilas, since you took your first step
into a glorious lifetime—
this, mixed with fame from
Kastor the chariot-driver,
hero who now, after winter's sharp storms,   10
brightens your hearth with well-being.

Wise men wear god-given
powers most nobly. You, walking in
justice, have blessedness as your companion;
you rule as king—   15
an inborn primacy, joined to your heart,
makes this its most sacred prize, and
now you are blessed once more
as, with your promise of
Pythian glory fulfilled by your   20
team, you give welcome to these men who
join in the victory dance—

ep. Apollo's delight! Do not forget,
you who are sung in Kyrana's sweet
    garden of Kypris, that always in all things a
god stands above as true cause!   25
Cherish Karrhotos,   the king's charioteer
best of companions, for never with Alibi,
Afterthought's slow-witted child,
did he return to the halls of the right-ruling Battiads!
No—from his stay at the spring of Kastalia   Delphi
he brought a chariot crown and   31
    twisted it into your hair!

2. Twelve fast courses he
drove in that precinct, reins never
cut; he damaged no part but hung up the
car as a gift,   35
its skilled metalwork just as it was when,
from Krisa's ridge, he
entered the god's hollow valley. It
hangs in the cypress-wood shrine,
close to the figure cut from a tree-trunk,   40
offered by archers of Crete and set in the
treasure-house there on Parnassos.

Give glad reception to
one who brings benefits! You,
o Alexibios' son, are lit by the   Karrhotos, above line 26
lovely haired Graces!   46
Blessed are you who, after strong toil, are
remembered with praise even stronger!
Where forty fell,
your fearless mind kept your   50
chariot whole and from glorious
strife you return to the Libyan plain and the
city your forefathers knew.

ep. No man is deprived of his portion of
toil, or ever will be, but Battos'   55

ancient good fortune persists, granting various
prizes. A guardian tower for the
city, for guests the
friendliest eye, bellowing lions
fled him in fear when they heard his   cf. P. 4.59–62 and Paus. 10.15.7
outlandish voice, for Apollo the founder of   60
colonies sent them great terror, that oracles
given to Kyrana's steward
    should not remain unfulfilled.

3. That god brings cures for grave
illness to men and to women;
he gives the lyre, bestowing the Muse where he   65
will and bringing
concord, war's enemy, into men's minds. He, from
his mantic cave, sent the
brave sons of Herakles and, too, the
heirs of Aigimios, to settle in   a legendary proto-Dorian
Argos, in Lakedaimon,   71
and in holy Pylos. I sing a
glory spreading from Sparta, the

land from which Aigeid
men, my forebears, crossed over to   75
Thera, not without heavenly aid but
led by some Fate.
From that place, o Apollo, we brought your
feast rich in sacrifice; now at the
Karneian table we   80
honor Kyrana, city built
high, where bronze-armored Trojans,
sons of Antenor, yet dwell. Bringing
Helen, they came when their own land was

ep. filled with the smoke of fires set by Ares.   85
That race of chariot drivers receives
    offerings and gifts from those who came
later with Battos, their ships

cutting a path through the
sea. He then broadened the groves of the gods   he=Battos
and, for Apollo's processions,   90
laid down a straight road, stone-paved and level,
ready to echo with sounding hooves, and
there, at the edge of the marketplace,
    he lies apart now, in death.

3. Blessed was he among
men, then worshipped as hero by   95
all of his people. Kings who came after, once
summoned to Hades,
rest at a distance beyond his door. Their buried
hearts perhaps listen as
acts of great courage are drenched in the   100
soft dew that's poured out by dancers—
glory and blessedness gained and
shared now with Arkesilas, their own son.
He, with this revel, rightly hails

Phoibos whose sword is of   105
gold, for it was at Pytho that
he earned this victory chant, our fair return for his
lavish expense!
Those who are wise give him praise and their words
I shall repeat: he keeps a   110
mind and a tongue that outpass his
years—in courage a long-winged
eagle, in contest a rampart! Since
childhood he soars with the Muses, while his
chariot skill has been witnessed.   115

ep. He dared to besiege each local portal of
fame and a favoring god brings his
    strength to perfection. O blessed children of
Kronos, grant to his future
deeds and designs the
same fine success! Let no autumn storm   120

injure his life with rough windblasts!
Zeus' great mind ever governs the fates of
men that he loves. I beg him now to
give, at Olympia, another such
    prize to the Battiad line!

PYTHIAN 6   The Rescue of Nestor

For Xenokrates of Akragas, a city on the southern coast of Sicily where the victor's older brother, Theron, ruled from 489 until 472 BC (see Olympians 2 and 3). The official ode for this chariot victory was made, according to ancient scholars, by the older poet, Simonides, and since the present song seems to have been intended for performance by a youthful chorus (note the reference to Aphrodite at the beginning), it may have been commissioned by or for the victor's son, the Thrasyboulos of line 18, who has just come of age (line 47). Some have supposed that he drove his father's chariot, but there is no evidence for this. For another ode for Xenokrates, made perhaps twenty years later, shortly after his death, and addressed to Thrasyboulos, see Isthmian 2.

The story of Antilochos' rescue of his father, Nestor, must come from a lost epic source; it does not appear in Homer, but Pindar could assume that it would be known to his Sicilian audience.
490 BC

1. Listen! We plough a field that belongs to the
    goddess with sparkling
eyes, Aphrodite, or else to the Graces! We
move toward the navel of rumbling earth
where—for the river-washed town of Akragas, the   5
prosperous Emmenids, and for Xenokrates—   Theron's family
a treasure-house stands in the gold-filled
gorge of Apollo, ready with hymns for a Pythian victor.

2. Never will winter's cold rains ravage that   10
    hall as an enemy force
striking from faraway clouds, nor will winds ever
carry it off in a silt-swirl to undersea caves!
Bathed in pure sunlight, its porch will
tell of a chariot victory known to men's tongues as   15

glorious—your father's, Thrasyboulos, taken in
Krisa's deep valley and shared with his clan!

3. Keeping him close on your right, you honor the   20
    law that, so they say,
high in the mountains the son of Philyra once   son=Chiron
gave to the powerful offspring of Peleus, orphaned and   Achilles
left in his care: Above other gods,
worship the loud-voiced Kronian master of thunder and
lightning and never, through all the length of their   25
lives, scant parents of reverence due!

4. Minding this rule, mighty Antilochos long ago   son of Nestor
    died in defense of his
father, under attack from the man-killing   30
Memnon, the dread Ethiopian prince. Trans-   cf. N. 3.63, 6.50; I. 5.41, 8.55
fixed by an arrow from Paris, Nestor's lead
horse had brought down his car and the enemy waited,
fondling his powerful spear. The old man of Messenē,   35
dazed in his heart, loudly cried out to his son,

5. nor did his voice fall unheard, for the other,
    like to a god, took his stand
and with his death bought his father's salvation.
His fearsome deed inspired awe and, by the   40
youths of that old generation, he was judged
first in honoring parents. But all this belongs to the
past—it's Thrasyboulos who among men of our day
best meets the standards of piety, while he yet   45

6. vies with his uncle in splendid display!   uncle=Theron
    His mind governs his
wealth as he harvests a youth neither rough nor unjust but
skilled in the ways of the Muses. You, o Poseidon,
earth-shaking master of every equestrian   50
contest, he follows, bringing you joy, while with
drinking companions his heart is more sweet
than is the chambered work of the bees!

PYTHIAN 7   An Athenian Exile

For Megakles of Athens, son of Hippokrates, nephew of Kleisthenes and uncle of Perikles. The Alkmaionid tribe (line 3) was one of Athens' richest and most distinguished; they had, in the mid sixth century, restored the temple of Apollo at Delphi (lines 10–11, cf. Herodotos 5.62), and they claimed many crowns from major contests (lines 11–16). Megakles had been ostracized in 487 BC (lines 18–19, cf. Aristotle, *Ath. pol.* 22), as a supporter of the heirs of the tyrant, Pisistratos, but in the following year he won at Delphi with his four-horse chariot. This modest and slightly embittered ode would have been performed in exile.
486 BC

1. Athens, great among cities, offers the
fairest foundation a man can lay down as
prelude to praise for the mighty Alkmaionids
and for their chariot teams! What homeland, what   5
house more honored in Hellas
could you proclaim as your own?

Tales of Erechtheus' descendants are told in all   early king of Athens
cities, Apollo, for they made your temple at
Pytho a wonder to see. The five crowns they
brought back from Isthmia guide me yet further,
as does that one, most superb, from   15
Zeus at Olympia, and the two

ep. taken at Kirrha, o Megakles—all of them yours or   Delphi
won by your forebears! This new success brings me
joy, but I grieve to see
envy responding to these splendid deeds. Still,
even where happiness blooms and abides, its   20
fruits, so men say, are of various sorts.

For Aristomenes of Aigina, son of Xenarkes (lines 19, 72) of the Meidylid clan; two uncles, probably his mother's brothers, have also been victors, Theognetos at Olympia and Kleitomachos at Nemea (lines 36–7). Aristomenes has won at Delphi in the boys' wrestling, as he did earlier at Megara and Marathon (lines 78–9), and he has also competed in the pentathlon at local games for Apollo and Artemis (lines 65–6). Lines 57–60 suggest that the victor's party stopped at a local shrine of Alkmaon, the son of Amphiaraos, as they were setting out for Delphi.

For other treatments of the two Argive expeditions led by Adrastos (line 49) against Thebes, the first of Fathers, the second of Sons (also called the Epigonoi, lines 40, 41), see Olympian 6.13–7 and Isthmian 7.10–11. In flight from Thebes, when the first attack was repulsed, Amphiaraos was swallowed up by the earth at what became his prophetic shrine (see Nemean 9.9–27); it is thus from underground that Amphiaraos speaks at lines 43–55.

To the powers of Tranquility, in the invocation, compare those of Apollo's lyre at the opening of Pythian 1.

This is perhaps the last ode that Pindar made; it seems to have been composed after the Athenian conquest of Aigina but before the terms of the Thirty Years' Peace were known.

446 BC

1. Kindly Tranquility, daughter of Justice,
you who make cities great, holding the
high keys of counsel and war,
welcome this Pythian prize-song
brought to you by Aristomenes!
Elegant leisure is yours; you know its
making, its taking, and its fitting hour!

Yet should anyone drive stubborn hatred
into his heart, you resist, thrusting his

Hesychia/Dika

5

99

insolence into the bilge.   10
This truth Porphyrion hadn't yet   *king of giants, line 16*
learned when he senselessly roused up your
anger! Yes, gain is a friend, should it
come from one willing to give, but in time the

ep. arrogant fall by their own brute force. Hundred-head   15
Typhon did not escape, nor did the king of the
giants, the one felled by the bolt, the other by   *Zeus' thunderbolt*
darts from Apollo—the same god who welcomed the
son of Xenarkes, come up from Kirrha with   *Delphi*
loud Doric mirth and wreathed in Parnassian laurel!   20

2. This island city devoted to justice
fell to a spot not far from the Graces, her   *as if cast like a game-piece*
contact with Aiakid deeds
lending primordial fame. She is
sung as the parent of heroes triumphant in   25
many a prize-bearing contest,
and as winner of swift-moving battles,

while her citizens too are admired. But
I haven't time to fit the full tale to soft
speech and the lyre, and would   30
fear lest glut might ensue. But this
debt that runs at my feet, boy, owed to your   *like a toy or animal?*
latest success—let it be gone,   *for song-debt, cf. O. 10.7–12*
carried away on my winged machine!

ep. Tracking your uncles into the ring, you do not   35
taint Theognetos' Olympian deed, nor do you
smirch Kleitomachos' bold Isthmian triumph!
Making the Meidylids strong, you merit the
words that the prophet proposed on seeing the   *Amphiaraos*
Sons, spears ready, at Thebes' seven gates.   40

3. The Epigonoi, just come from Argos, had
opened the second attack and he spoke as they fought:

"High courage, bred in the
bone, shines out by nature in
father and son! I see him clearly   45
—Alkmaon—his shield's spotted snake   son of Amphiaraos
first in the strife at the Kadmaean gates!

He who endured the former attempt, the
hero Adrastos, now has a   cf. O. 6.13–17
happier omen, though   50
worse for his family hearth: only
he out of all the Greek host will sift earth for the
bones of a son then, aided by
heaven, return—army unharmed—to the

ep. broad streets of Abbas." Amphiaraos so spoke, and   Argos
I too rejoice as I sprinkle Alkmaon with   56
hymns and tossed crowns, for he, my neighbor and keeper of
treasure, appeared on the road to the song-filled
navel of earth and there prophesied,   Delphi
using the skills that he had from his father.   60

4. And, o far-shooter, lord of the famed and   Apollo
welcoming shrine in the Pythian glade, it was
there that you gave this
greatest of joys, as earlier,
closer to home, at the festival   65
shared with your sister, you granted the coveted
pentathlon prize! Be pleased, o lord, to

look with harmonious glance upon my every
step! Justice stands close to this
sweet-singing throng and   70
I ask the gods, o Xenarkēs, to
keep an unjealous eye on your
fortunes! He who succeeds without drudgery
seems to the many a wise man surrounded by

ep. fools, crowning his life by his knowing contrivance, but   75
such things are not in man's power. God ever prevails—
tossing one up, overwhelming another, he   like an umpire
enters the ring to keep order. You won at Megara, as on
Marathon's plain, and here at home in Hera's games
you, Aristomenes, triumphed three times!   80

5. Four bodies you fell upon, meaning dire harm,
nor were they granted returns such as
yours by the Pythian judges.
Finding their mothers, no sweet
laughter awakened delight—they came   85
dodging their enemies, skulking up
alleys, gnawed by misfortune's sharp bite.

He who has as his lot fresh success meanwhile
soars in soft luxury, raised up by
hope and floating on   90
pinions of manliness, thoughts aimed
far beyond wealth. Yet such mortal joy,
swift in its growth, as swiftly falls to the
ground, shaken by harsh premonition.

ep. We live for a day. Someone, no one—what are they?   95
Man is the dream of a shade but when god-given
splendor descends, light rests upon all and a
sweet life-span. Dear mother Aigina,
pilot this city toward freedom, with Zeus, lord Aiakos,
Peleus, Achilles, and brave Telamon in our convoy!   100

For Telesikrates, son of Karneiadas, of Cyrene (Kyrana) in Libya, victor in
the heavy-armed race in which helmeted men wearing greaves and carry-
ing shields ran 200 yards. (For other odes performed in Cyrene, see
Pythians 4 and 5.) A scholiast reports a statue of an armed Telesikrates at
Delphi and lines 91–2 seem to say that he was the first athlete from
Cyrene to win in a Panhellenic contest; lines 79–84 suggest that he has
also taken a crown at the Theban Iolaia, and the mythic section, like the
closing stanzas (lines 105–125), suggests that the victor has recently
come to the age at which men married.
474 BC ?

1. Aided by deep-waisted Charites,   Graces
I would proclaim Telesikrates—blessed man—as
shield-bearing Pythian victor and bringer of glory to
chariot-driving Kyrana! That nymph, a
maid yet untamed, was ravished from Pelion's echoing   5
    valleys by long-haired Apollo, who
carried her off in his golden car,
setting her down in a land filled with
fruit trees and flocks in abundance, to
dwell there as queen at the flourishing
    root of a third continent.   cf. P. 4.15

Silver-shod Kypris welcomed her   Aphrodite
Delian visitor, touching his god-made chariot   10
lightly and sprinkling his sweet marriage-couch with a reverent
awe as she yoked them in wedlock—the god and the
daughter of violent Hypseos. (That was the hero who
    ruled at the time over arrogant
Lapiths, the grandson of Ocean but
born in the glorious valley of
Pindos to Kreusa, a naiad who

first tasted joy in the bed of the   16
    river-god Peneios, she the

ep. daughter of Gē.) Hypseos nourished the
fair-armed Kyrana in childhood but she had no
    taste for the journeying shuttle
nor for stay-at-home suppers with friends.
Rather, with spear or the blade of her sword, she would   20
challenge wild beasts, then
slaughter them, bringing a tranquil
safety and peace to her father's herds.
Scant time she spent with that
sweet bedmate, sleep, as it
settled toward dawn on her eyelids!   25

3. Once, as she fought with a furious
lion, unarmed and alone, Apollo the far-shooter
chanced to see. He straightaway shouted to Chiron, "O
son of Philyra! Come out from your sacred and
cavernous halls to marvel with me at the courage and   30
    excellent strength of this girl—
see how she keeps a cool head as she fights,
heart in command of her work, her
wits not frozen by fear!
What mortal parent has she? From whose
    house was she taken to

dwell in these shadowy mountains
testing her unrestrained boldness? Would it be god-like, were   35
my famous hand to reach out and pluck the sweet
grass from her bed?" The spirited Centaur
gave a quick smile, lifted an eyebrow, and spoke his
    mind: "Phoibos, the keys to
all sacred loves are wisely kept secret by
Peitho. This is forbidden by   Persuasion
shame among gods as among   40
men—to enter a sweet virgin
    couch in broad daylight! But

ep. surely soft passion has twisted your speech, for
you by decree cannot touch an untruth. Do
    you, my lord, ask the girl's ancestors—
you who know the sure end of all things
and the way? You can number the springtime   45
sprouts that earth sends, the
sand-grains that move in river or
sea, driven by waves and by wind!
    You know the future and
whence it will come, but if
I am to rival such wisdom, I'll   50

3. speak. You are come to this vale as her
mate; you will carry her over the sea to a splendid
garden belonging to Zeus and there, leading men from an
island to settle the hill on the plain, you will   island=Thera, cf. P. 4 and 5
give her the rule of a city. On this very day,   55
    Libya, lady of broad fields, will
joyously welcome her into a
palace of gold as your bride! A   cf. lines 7–12
portion of earth will be lawfully
hers, nor will it lack in
    fruit-bearing trees or wild beasts.

She will give birth to a son whom
Hermes will take from his mother and carry aloft to   60
Gē and the Hours, seated on high, and they, with the
babe on their knees, will drip nectar into his
mouth, and ambrosia, making him deathless—like Zeus or
    holy Apollo! Dear to his
mortal companions as guardian of
flocks, for some he'll be Nomos, for
others Agrios or Aristaios."   as protector of flocks and the hunt
So he urged the god on toward the   65
    pleasure-filled marital goal.

ep. Action is swift and short is the road when a
god is in haste. That day sufficed; they became

one in Libya's gold-filled
chamber—here in the city now hers,
fairest and known for its contests! So, with his   70
Pythian crown, does the
son of Karneiadas now
marry the bloom of his fortune to hers, and she   she=Kyrana
   welcomes him gladly, for
he, to this land of fair
women, brings his Delphic fame!   75

4. Great deeds attract many tales but the
wise would hear brevity fashioned from length. Always the
summit belongs to the opportune moment. Seven-gate
Thebes saw this truth not dishonored when with the   79
tip of his sword Iolaos sliced off the   nephew of Herakles
   head of Eurystheus. They   king who persecuted Herakles
laid him away in the tomb of the chariot-
driver, Amphitryon, his father's father,   cf. N. 4.20 and 10.13–17
come long ago as a guest of the
Spartoi to dwell in the Kadmeian
   streets where white horses run.

Coupled with him and with Zeus, Alk-   84
mena the wise with one birth-pang bore two   Herakles and Iphikles
   sons, both
masters of battle. He must be dumb who won't use his   cf. N. 1
lips in Herakles' praise or mention the
waters of Dirka where Iphikles drank! My prayer well
   answered, I dance for them now.
May the pure light of the echoing
Charites never desert me, for
I say that thrice—at Aigina   90
and on Nisos' hill—you brought   at Megara
   glorious praise to this city. Your

ep. exploits contriving escape from an
impotent silence. No citizen, friend or   lack of fame=lack of power
   enemy ever should hide

work done well in the interest of all.
That would defy the rule of old Nereus: Praise   95
even your foe, justly, and from the heart,
should he perform a fine deed!
Unmarried girls, Telesikrates,
    seeing you crowned at the
contests for Pallas, have   local games
silently prayed for a like   100

5. husband or son—so too at our local
Olympics, our games for deep-breasted Earth, and at
all of the nearby trials! Song-thirst now quenched, a
duty commands me to waken the fame of those
ancestors who, for the sake of a Libyan woman,   105
    went long ago to the city of
Irasa, seeking the hand of Antaios'
famed and lovely-haired daughter; she was a
bride sought by many fine men, some
kinsmen and some from abroad, for her
    beauty was splendid to see.

All wished to pluck gold-crowned Hebē's ripe
fruit but her father, wanting a rite more worthy of   110
note, thought on Danaos—how, once in long ago Argos,
he had arranged the swiftest of nuptials for
forty-eight daughters, all before noon, by placing the
    troupe at the term of a racecourse and
setting a contest, with the injunction that
swiftness of foot should determine
which of the girls should be   115
won by which of the heroes
    gathered to court them.

ep. Such too was the Libyan's mode in matching a   Antaios (line 106)
groom to his girl. He arrayed her and set her as
    prize at the end of a course, then to
all he announced that he who leapt forward and
first touched her robe might take her as bride.   120

It was Alexidamos, the
best in a swift field, whose
hand took the maid's to lead her away
   through mounted Nomads. Many the
garlands they tossed!—many the
plumes he had already taken!   125

PYTHIAN 10   Perseus among the Hyperboreans

For Hippokleas of Pelinna, a city in the northern region of Thessaly, winner in the boys' double-stade race (about 400 yards). The boy is the son of an Olympian victor, Phrikias (lines 12–16, 20–28), but the ode has been commissioned by the local prince, Thorax (line 63), probably because Hippokleas was a special favorite.

The youthful Perseus was challenged by the lord of Seriphos to bring him the snake-haired head of the Medusa, whose glance could turn man or beast to stone, and with Athena's help he succeeded (see Pythian 12); on his way back he found himself in the legendary region behind the home of the north wind.

According to scholars of antiquity, this was the earliest of Pindar's surviving odes, composed when he was about twenty years old.
498 BC

1. Happy is Lakedaimon, blessed is Thessaly—
both take their rulers from Herakles' line,
he who was bravest in battle!
Do I boast out of turn? No—Pelinna and
    Pytho demand it, as do the
sons of Aleuas, eager to   *local ruling house*
praise Hippokleas with revel and song.   6

He likes the flavor of contest! Parnassos' hollow has
sounded his name to the neighboring host as
best in the boys' two-stade race.
Among mortals, Apollo, the end proves   10
    sweet when a god calls the start! He
won by your will but heredity
set him upon the path of his father, for

ep. Phrikias twice was Olympian victor in
full battle dress, while the contest   *the heavy-armed race (hoplitodromos)*

held beneath Kirrha's high cliffs   at Delphi
made him supreme among runners.   16
May destiny grant to their latter
days noble wealth that comes to full flower.

2. Not scant is their portion of Hellenic pleasures—let
no angry god send reversal! One whose   20
heart knew no pain would be god, but
happy and worthy of poets' songs is
    he who has conquered by virtue of
hands or swift feet, has taken the
greatest of crowns with boldness and strength, then

lived on to watch his young son capture a Pythian   25
wreath as his due. Heaven's bronze floor is
not his to walk but his voyage
reaches the outermost term of those glories that
    mortals may touch. Going by
ship or by foot, you'll not discover the
path to the land beyond Boreas, where   30

ep. Perseus, leader of men, once entered and
dined, welcomed by hosts who
sacrificed hundreds of asses.
Apollo ever takes joy in such
feasting and worship and laughs at the   35
towering lust of the beasts they cut down,

3. nor does the Muse shun such rites. Everywhere maidens in
chorus, lyre-tones, and cries from the flute
circle about, while with golden
laurel-leaves bound in their hair, citizens   40
    celebrate. Illness and wretched old
age cannot touch this sanctified
race—they live without battle or toil,

safely escaped from the rulings of Nemesis.   divine anger at excess; cf. 20
Led by Athena and breathing with bold heart, the

son of Danaë was welcomed by   45
this blessed crowd; he had slaughtered the
   Gorgon and now brought her head with its
serpentine locks—death made of stone—
back to the men of the island. For   *Seriphos, where crowds would be petrified*

ep. me, no marvel achieved by the gods can be
open to disbelief.   50
Stop oars—drop the prow anchor into the
depths and guard against bristling
reefs, for a victory hymn at its best
flits like a bee from one tale to the next!

4. As men of Ephyra here beside Peneios   55
pour out my song, I hope, thanks to his
crowns, to make Hippokleas
yet more admired among elders and
   friends, while for unmarried
girls he becomes a compelling concern!
Different loves tease different minds, but   60

whatever each may pursue, if caught, let him
keep it clutched tightly, for no sign can tell
all that a year's turn may bring. I
trust the warm welcome of Thorax who, quick to
   further my purpose, readied the
car of the Muses and willingly led out this leader!   65

ep. Tried on a touchstone, gold shines out,
as does an upright
mind. Two fine brothers we praise, men who   *brothers of Thorax*
strengthen the order of Thessaly where   70
civic rule rests with the
nobles—a cherished inherited power.

For Thrasydaios of Thebes, a city in Boiotia (where Pindar was born), son of Pythonikos, and winner of the boys' footrace; his father was also a Pythian victor (note lines 14 and 43–50), and another forebear seems to have taken a chariot crown at Olympia (lines 46–8). Thrasydaios was probably about twelve years old, for according to the scholiasts he won a men's title twenty years later.

The opening lines call upon a set of goddesses and local heroines to join Apollo's Theban bride Melia (line 4) in his sanctuary to celebrate the present victory (lines 9–14). Mention of the Ismenion (named for Apollo's son, Ismenos, line 6) suggests the Theban ritual of the Daphnephoria, with its boy leader, girls' chorus, and golden tripods (line 4, cf. Pausanias 9.10.4), and it seems probable that young Thrasydaios has recently served, or will soon serve, as its prime figure, the Daphnephoros or laurel-bearer.

Scholars both ancient and modern have condemned the mythic section of this ode as worse than irrelevant, and the singers call attention to their daring choice of Klytaimnestra (lines 37–8), but her wifely betrayal is here used to emphasize the filial loyalty of the young Orestes who avenges his father as soon as he has come of age (lines 30–6).
474 BC

1. You daughters of Kadmos—Semelē, housed with Olympian
powers, and Ino who shares the
    Nereids' chamber—go now with
Herakles' mother, best maker of sons, to join Melia
    there in the shrine of the golden tripods, the
treasure-house Loxias honored by calling it   5

Ismenion—throne-room of true divination.   cf. Pausanias 9.10.4
There, o Harmonia's children,   wife of Kadmos
    he now summons a conclave of
all local heroines. As night descends, you are to

112

celebrate Themis the holy, sing Pytho
and too the right-judging navel of Earth,   10

ep. as you bring grace to seven-gate Thebes and the
contest at Kirrha, for there Thrasydaios   Delphi
reminded the world of his father's hearth by
casting a third crown upon it,
won in the rich fields of Pylades,   15
friend to Orestes of Lakedaimon.

2. Him, while his father lay bloodied, Arsinoë saved from the
powerful hands and cruel plots
     of Klytaimnestra when, with her
polished blade, she sent Kassandra, the daughter of Priam,
     along with the spirit of king Agamemnon,
down to the deep-shaded banks of the Acheron—   20

pitiless woman! Was it Iphigeneia, her throat
slashed far from home at Euripos, that
     caused her to let loose her
ponderous rage? Or did those nights spent in the bed of her   25
     paramour lead her astray? For a young wife
this is a most hateful crime, not easily

ep. hidden from gossiping tongues, since
neighbors are given to talk. Great wealth brings
envy as great, while he who lies low can
rumble unnoticed. The Atreid hero   Agamemnon
died when at last he returned to his   31
splendid Amyklai, destroying the mantic

3. maiden as well—he who for Helen's sake robbed burning   line 19
Troy of its wealth! But his son, still a
     babe, was sent to old Strophios
under Parnassos and, aided by Ares, in time he   35
     cut down the mother and
settled Aigisthos in his own gore.

But o my friends, have I strayed at a crossing to lose the straight
path that I followed? Or does some
   storm-wind drive me off course like the
frailest of ships? Muse, yours is the task!   40
   Hired out for silver, your voice must
move in disorder toward subjects that shift—now

ep. touching the sire, Pythonikos, now treating the
son, Thrasydaios, both blazing with fame and
festive good cheer. As chariot victors in   45
fabled Olympian contests, their
horse-driving forebears
seized a swift brilliance and these two at

4. Pytho entered the foot-race and shamed all gathered
Greeks with their speed. I would wish   50
   only for god-given goods as I
seek what my years shall propose. I find blessedness
   flowering best in the city's
mid-ranks—the lot of the tyrant I fault as I

reach toward the common good. This wards off envy.
If, gaining the heights, a man rests there in   55
   quietude, spurning all insolence,
his term of black death grows more fair as, to
   kinsmen he loves, he bequeaths the
best of possessions—a name that bears honor.

ep. So Iphikles' son, Iolaos, is chosen as   nephew and companion of Herakles
worthy of hymns, as are strong Kastor and   60
you, princely Pollux, heroes who   cf. N. 10
one day sit throned at Therapnē,
then on the next find your
home high in Olympian halls!

PYTHIAN 12 The Song of the Gorgon Sisters

For Midas of Akragas, in Sicily, the city of Theron (see Olympian 2), winner of the contest for performers on the pipe or *aulos*, a reed instrument something like an oboe. Such contests were held only at Delphi.

When Danaë and the newborn Perseus (fathered by Zeus in the form of a shower of gold) were locked in a chest and cast into the sea by her father, they washed up on the island of Seriphos, where they lived with a fisherman until Perseus came of age. Then the ruler Polydektes made Danaë his concubine and commanded Perseus to bring him the head of the Medusa. The task should have been impossible since the glance of a Gorgon could turn anyone to stone, but Athena intervened, and Perseus was able to take the monstrous head and eventually use it against Polydektes, rescuing his mother. For another treatment of the tale of Perseus, see Pythian 10.

490 BC

1. Fairest of all mortal cities, lover of splendor,
throne of Persephonē, you who dwell on an urban hill
close by the banks of the river Akragas where sheep feed, I
beg you, o mistress, rejoice in this Pythian crown
brought with the goodwill of men and of gods   5
by well-famed Midas! Receive him, strongest of Greeks in the
art that Pallas Athena contrived, twisting into its
fabric the harsh complaint of the fierce Gorgon sisters,

2. heard as it poured with laborious pain from the snake-heads of
those unapproachable virgins when Perseus cried out in   10
triumph and seized the third sister, to carry her off, as their
doom, to the sea-bound people of Seriphos. He
blinded the weird race of Phorkos, brought
misery into the banquet where sat Polydektes, and
ended his mother's forced service in slavery's couch when he   15
severed the head of the broad-cheeked Medusa—he, the

3. son of Danaë, said to have come from a free-fall of
gold! When Pallas had rescued her favorite mortal,
that maiden-goddess invented a many-voiced strain for the
pipe, that the plangent lament that had burst from the   20
clenched jaws of Euryalē might be   sister of Medusa
echoed by instruments. She, its first maker, meant it for
mortals and called it the "many-head mode," famed as
summons to contests where crowds of men gather, its

4. melody moving through channels of thin bronze and reeds   25
found in the nymph's precinct, close to the Charites' city of   Orchomenos;
fine public spaces—witnesses trusted by dancers.   cf. O. 14
If any blessedness comes among men it does not appear without
toil but sooner or later some Power will   30
make it complete; fate can't be escaped. A moment will
come that plays with surprises, tossing up
one boon against expectation, denying another.

The Birth of Herakles

For Chromios of Syracuse, son of Hagesidamos and victor in the chariot race; for another chariot victory of his, see Nemean 9. Chromios was the brother-in-law of Hieron, ruler of Syracuse, who appointed him governor of the recently founded Aitna (line 7, cf. Pythian 1) during the minority of Deinomenes, its intended king. This ode may have been performed on Ortygia (line 2), an island just off Syracuse where a spring sacred to Artemis had been created, according to legend, when the river god Alpheos took his first breath, after passing under the Ionian Sea in pursuit of that goddess. A scholiast reported statues of both Chromios and Hieron on Ortygia.
476 BC ?

1. Most sacred spot where Alpheos once caught his breath—
Ortygia, offshoot of glorious Syracuse,
Artemis' couch and
sister of Delos—our sweet-spoken hymn   birthplace of Artemis and Apollo
sets out from you, its aim to build praise for a   5
wind-swift team as a gift to the
    Aitnaian Zeus! Chromios' chariot,
Nemea too, urge us to yoke up our
    revel to prize-winning deeds.

So the foundation is laid using gods as its fabric, its
motive the heaven-sent prowess of this man. The
peak of all glory is   10
reached in triumphant success. The Muse
loves to remember great contests, so let's
scatter some splendor over the isle that
    Zeus, heaven's ruler, gave to
Persephonē, nodding his head as he
    vowed to exalt this most fruitful

ep. land, this rich Sicily, crowned with her   15
   high and luxurious cities!
He, Kronos' son, then supplied men,
   lovers of bronze-clashing war and
masters of horse who time and again wore
   garlands of golden Olympian
olive. I seize the moment of promise,
   nor do I make a false cast!   *as if the song were a javelin*

2. Here at the gates of a man who loves guests I
sing of fine deeds where a generous banquet is spread—   20
these halls are not without
knowledge of visiting strangers come
frequently and from afar! Those who would
fault noble men are fated to douse rich smoke with
   water. Mortals have various   *i.e., they treat the wrong object*
skills; best is to walk a straight path, in   25
   strife using powers inborn.

Strength tells in action, wisdom in counsel where
foresight resides as a gift from one's fathers and
you, by nature, use both,
   o son of Hagesidamos!
Great wealth kept hidden away in a palace I   30
do not desire; I would rather enjoy what
   riches I have while hearing the
thanks of my gratified friends.
   All men who toil have

ep. hopes of the same sort. I, as I   *all expect good and bad*
   treat of magnificent deeds,
eagerly seize upon Herakles,
   choosing that old tale of how, when he
fled from the pangs of his mother's womb   35
   into the sudden brilliance of
day—this son of Zeus with his brother and
   twin—to lie there in

3. saffron-dyed cradle clothes, he was not unobserved by
Hera whose throne is of gold. The gods' queen, with
rage in her heart, sent
two serpents down and they, when the   40
doors were flung open, entered the spacious birth-
chamber, mad to stretch their swift
   jaws round the infants, but Herakles
lifted his head, held it upright, and
   faced his first trial of battle, his

two inescapable hands seizing the snakes by their
throats. As they choked, time forced the   45
last gasp of life
from their unspeakable forms. At Alkmena's couch, the
women who watched were stricken with fear beyond
bearing, but she, the new mother,
   threw off her sheets and leapt to her feet,
unclothed but ready to fight off the   50
   serpents' outrageous attack.

ep. Kadmeian leaders ran up in a throng
   armed with bronze weapons, Amphitryon
with them, grasping a naked
   sword in his hands and smitten with
sharp agony. All men are struck by the
   weight of familial misfortune but
hearts soon recover from griefs
   brought by another man's trouble.

4. He stood confounded, his terror mingled with   55
joy for he saw the inordinate temper and
strength of his son—the
gods had countered the messenger's words! He
summoned his neighbor—Teiresias, speaker of
truth and first among prophets of   60
   Zeus the most high, who announced to
him and all present what fortunes the
   child was destined to meet:

how many lawless beasts he would slay on dry land,
how many others at sea! He told of
one who would prey upon   Antaios? Busiris?
men as he followed his crooked path, and of the   65
odious doom that would find him. He promised that
whenever gods should do battle with
    giants on Phlegra's plain, locks of bright
hair would lie grimed in dust under the
    onslaught of this hero's shafts.

ep. Last, he foretold that these mighty
    labors would bring in return
unbroken quiet and peace, en-   70
    joyed through all time in a palace of
blessedness where, with ripe Hebē as bride, he would
    dine at his wedding feast seated with
Zeus, son of Kronos, and praising the
    hallowed rule of his father.

For Timodemos of Acharnai in Attica, victor in the pankration, son of
Timonoös whose family, the Timodemids, had settled on the island of
Salamis (line 13). This seems to be Timodemos' first success (lines 3–5),
but his clan already held a record of nineteen crowns from the major
games (though none from Olympia).
Sometime before 480 BC

1. As singers descended from Homer
open their stitched recitations with
Zeus as a prelude, so this man begins at the
much-hymned precinct of Nemean Zeus,
    making a pledge of
victories yet to be taken in crown games.   5

2. His debt still stands, for if the fate that
marks the straight path of his fathers would
give him to Athens as proud decoration,
he must many times pluck the fair Isthmian
    prize, and be a
Pythian victor, as offspring of Timonoös!   10

3. This follows, much as Orion the
mountain-born followed the Pleiads —
not far behind! Salamis truly can nurture a
fighter, for Hektor at Troy paid Ajax some   *Il.* 7.287 ff.
    heed. O Timodemos,
your strong pankratic boldness exalts you!   15

4. Ancient report makes Acharnai a
land of brave men and in athletic talk
first to be hailed are the Timodemids. From the
throne of Parnassos they brought four crowns

and Korinth has
joined them with eight, won in the   20

5. folds of lord Pelops' domain, while
seven were taken at Nemea, others past
number at home in the contest for Zeus. O
citizens, dance for that god as you
    hail Timodemos' return—
raise a sweet sound and celebrate him!   25

NEMEAN 3   The Childhood of Achilles

For Aristokleidas of the island of Aigina, son of Aristophanes and victor in the boys' pankration. The victor's family evidently held a hereditary position at the Aiginetan temple of Pythian Apollo (line 70), and the ode, which was delivered late (lines 5, 79), seems to have been performed in the temple courtyard.

Aiakos, son of Zeus and the nymph Aigina, was highly honoured on Aigina, and he and/or his descendants figure in all of the songs that Pindar made for this island; note the singers' self-exhortation here at lines 28–36, with the summary that follows, and compare the mythic subjects of Nemeans 4, 5, 6, 7, and 8 and Isthmians 5, 6, and 8.
475 BC ?

1. Mother of singers, sovereign Muse, I beg you
now in the sacred Nemean month—come to this
guest-loving Aigina, Doric isle!
Here beside Asopos' waters young
craftsmen of sweetly sung revels are waiting,   5
mad for a signal from you. Each deed has its
separate thirst and triumph in contest craves song, best
comrade of courage and crowns, so

send an abundance, drawn from my skill! You are his
daughter—open a laud for the ruler of heaven and   Zeus
I will set parts for these echoing   11
voices and for the lyre! Sweet
work will be theirs as pride of a land where
Myrmidons dwell, for Aristokleidas
(aided by you) brought no stain of dishonor to   15
their meeting ground when tested in

ep. stubborn pankratic company. Sung in the deep
meadows at Nemea, the victory strain puts

123

poultice to injuries suffered there.
Fair in himself, Aristophanas' boy matched his
beauty with deeds and climbed to the summit of   20
    courage—none can readily
enter the untried sea beyond Herakles' pillars,

2. boundaries set by that hero-god, marking the
sailor's uttermost stretch. He mastered proud
maritime beasts and alone charted the
shallows, mapped out the land, then   25
touched at the end that fixed his return.
But, o my heart, why beach me on this far shore?
Carry my Muse to Aiakos and to his race, for
justice says: Praise what is noble!

Nor are exotic ambitions the best—seek closer home!   30
Fit decoration for sweet song is part of your
portion. Peleus, shaping his
conquering shaft, rejoiced in old
virtues—he who alone and bereft of his
army took Iolkos, then gave ocean-born   35
Thetis a fall! Fighting beside Iolaos, fierce
Telamon finished Laomedon, then

ep. followed his friend against bronze-armed Amazon
archers, nor did fright ever stop him or
    blunt his resolve. Inborn glory gives
weight to a man while the one whose virtues have   40
merely been learned pants after random things
    blindly, his foot never sure as he
senselessly samples ten-thousand glorious deeds.

3. Pale-haired Achilles, still in the care of Philyra,   mother of Chiron
toyed with bold deeds, a mere child, twirling his small spear, then
sending it swift as the wind to bloody the   45
coats of furious lions
or to kill boar. When he was six he
carried his first gasping corpses back to the

Kronian centaur and this he continued to do;   Chiron
Athena and Artemis marvelled to   50

see him take deer, not with entangling nets or with
dogs, but racing on his own two feet! Mine is an
old tale—how in his troglodyte cave
deep-thinking Chiron housed Jason,   cf. P. 4.102–5
Asklepios too, teaching the soothing practice of   cf. P. 3.45–6
pharmacy. He gave Thetis of glorious   56
womb to her husband and cared for her powerful son,   Achilles
training his temper in fit ways, so that

ep. once sent to Troy by gusting sea-winds he might
stand and resist the Dardanian war-cry, the   60
     Phrygian and Lydian too, and then,
mixed in close combat with Ethiope warriors, might
hammer this purpose into his will:
     "No going home for the furious
Memnon, Helenos' cousin, their   cf. P. 6.32; N. 6.50; I. 5.41, 8.54
          mightiest lord!"

4. Such is the source of the far-reaching light of the
Aiakids. Yours, Zeus, is the blood, yours the contest   65
tossed by this hymn to the voices of boys to be
sung as a local joy! Shouts suit
Aristokleidas, victor whose triumph adds
fame to this isle and splendid concerns to the
sanctified house of the Pythian envoys. In   70
mid-trial fulfillment shines out where one is

meant for preeminence, be he child among children,
man among men, or in the third age, an elder—
just as his mortal lot may ordain.
Fate holds four virtues in harness, the   courage, good counsel,
last being care for what lies at hand, and   justice, concentration
not one is absent today! Farewell, my friend. I
offer this musical sip of honey and white milk,
dew-frothed and borne (a bit late) on the

ep. breath of Aiolian pipes! Swift is the eagle when   80
after a long chase he suddenly sinks his sharp
    claws in his blood-smeared prey while the
chattering jackdaws huddle below. Now
Kleio has willed, because of your prize-taking   Muse of fame
    temper, that light from Nemea,
Megara and Epidauros should shine upon you!

For Timasarchos of Aigina, of the Theandrid tribe, son of Timokritos (now dead, lines 13–15), grandson of Euphanes, and nephew on his mother's side of Kallikles, a deceased Isthmian victor (lines 80, 87–8). Timasarchos has won in the boys' wrestling; his trainer, the Athenian Milesias, was much admired among Aiginetans (cf. Olympian 8.54–64 and Nemean 6.65).

Exiled after the killing of Phokos (see Nemean 5), Peleus was chosen as the bridegroom of Thetis (this is the "destiny Zeus had determined," line 61, see Isthmian 8) because of the piety shown in his refusal of advances made by the wife of his host, Akastos (lines 57–9); nevertheless, he was able to take Thetis only after a wrestling match in which she exercised her powers as a form-changer. About to describe this match, the boy singers make fun of themselves as unable to resist the lure of grandiose tales (lines 33–41); then a summary of Aiakid heroes (lines 46–52) leads to Peleus. In lines 90–92, the making of an (imaginary) ode for the trainer, Melesias, is likened to a wrestling match.
473 BC?

1. Joy is best healer, once toil is judged! Songs
artfully made, daughters of Muses,
charm as they touch, nor can warm water
bring to tired limbs such comfort as praise does,
mixed with the voice of the lyre. Cast into   5
speech, fame lives longer than deeds when—
touched by the Graces—the tongue
draws from the depths of the heart.

2. Such is the praise I would offer to Zeus, to
Nemea, and Timasarchos'   10
skill in the ring, as my hymn's prelude!
May it be welcome here at this towering
Aiakid seat, beacon of justice for strangers!

If Timokritos your father still felt the sun's
warmth, he would finger his lyre,   15
lean to the tune, and join in our

3. hymn for a son who sends a mixed garland of
crowns won at Kleonai and, too, at
famed and luxurious Athens. In
seven-gate Thebes near Amphitryon's tomb he was   20
joyously pelted with flowers by
Kadmeian men in honor of Aigina when, as
friend among friends, he gazed
down on the blest hall of Herakles.

4. With him strong Telamon once conquered Troy, the   him=Herakles
Meropēs, and that most fearsome   26
enemy, Alkyoneus, though not before
he, with one stone, smashed twelve chariots, each with four
horses and two hero drivers!
He who can't take my point knows little of   30
battle, where injury wrought is
apt to return to the doer.

5. Custom prohibits a lengthy account, as do the
hastening hours, but my heart is drawn as
if by a love-charm, to touch upon   35
grandeurs. Though the sea swirls at the ship's waist,
we can arrive in the light, all plots
resisted and stronger than rivals, while from the
shadows the envious man
tosses his platitudes out, to   40

6. fall to the ground. Of this I am sure—what
destiny grants creeping time will complete.
Weave, then, sweet lyre, this present song—
mix in a Lydian harmony, making it
dear to Oinona and pleasing to   Oinona=Aigina
Kypros where Teukros, Telamon's son, rules in   46

exile while Ajax keeps Salamis
as his inherited fief.

7. Off in the Black Sea Achilles holds his shining
isle; Thetis rules Phthia and, on the   50
cattle-rich heights that stretch from Dodona
down to the sea, Neoptolemos reigns. At   cf. N. 7.35–40
Pelion's foot lies Iolkos,
given by Peleus' militant hand
into Thessalian rule, after he'd   55
dealt with the sly and ingenious

8. schemes of Hippolyta, wife to Akastos.
That lord had plotted an ambushed death for his
guest, to be wrought by Daidalos' knife, but,
rescued by Chiron, Peleus met with the   60
destiny Zeus had determined.
Fire all-devouring, sharp claws of bold lions,
dread biting edges of most fearsome
teeth—these Peleus endured, then

9. married that high-throned Nereid girl! He   Thetis
saw the high circle of chairs where   66
rulers of sky and sea sat, offering
power and gifts meant for his race. But
no man may pass to the west of Cadiz.
Let's come about and make for the dry land of   70
Europe—the Aiakid tale is
too vast for me to explore. I

10. come to Theandrids as herald and witness of
limb-stretching games held at Olympia,
Isthmia, and Nemea, whence they return,   75
tested in strength and not without fame-laden
crowns. Timasarchos, a rumor calls
your clan the viceroy of victory's songs!

If, for Kallikles, your mother's
brother, you ask a monument   80

11. whiter than Parian marble, know this! Polished
gold catches each passing gleam but a
song of fine deeds gives a man bliss like
that of a king. May he yet, where he rests beside   he=Kallikles
Acheron, take in the sound of my voice as it   85
sings in this place where, in games for the thunderous
god of the trident, he too once
bloomed with Korinthian parsley!

12. He was sung in the past by Euphanes, your
grandfather, boy! Each has his own set of   90
age-mates and best describes those he has
faced. But to sing of Melesias would be a trial—   the boy's trainer
twisting one's phrases, hoping while
unthrown to grasp with a word, gentle to
good men but waiting and ready to   95
grapple with those of ill will!

For Pytheas, from the island of Aigina, son of Lampon of the Psalychiad
tribe, and victor in the pankration for boys under fifteen (lines 6–7).
Since the paternal family had until now produced no crown victors, Lam-
pon evidently requested that this ode should include praise for Euthy-
menes, his wife's brother (line 39), for Themistios, her father (line 51),
and also for the boy's trainer, the Athenian Milesias (lines 64–6).

The Aiginetans defined themselves as creatures of their island, not of
the sea, with a complex myth that joined Zeus with the nymph Aigina to
engender a godlike Aiakos (cf. Isthmian 8.16.25; Nemean 8.6), to whom
two brides were assigned. The first of these, Psammathē, daughter of
Okeanos, gave birth to Phokos (line 11), part seal and part man; the second,
Endaïs, an earth power (line 10), produced a pair of fully human sons,
Peleus and Telamon, who when they came of age destroyed their watery
half-brother, went into exile, pursued many adventures, and fathered two
more Aiakid heroes, Achilles (the father of Neoptolemos) and Ajax.

The opening lines may refer to the pedimental sculptures depicting
the two campaigns against Troy that decorated the recently refurbished
temple of Aphaia at Aigina.
Ca. 483 BC

1. I am no sculptor whose works stand
    idle upon their base!
Go forth, sweet song, with every
    vessel or merchant bark—
set sail from Aigina bearing the news that
Pytheas, Lampon's strong son, takes a
pankratic garland at Nemea, though not   5
yet has he shown to his mother
    any soft bloom on his cheek!

He honors spear-bearing Aiakids
    fathered by Zeus and

Kronos upon golden Nereids,
   honors his city, too, as
friendly to strangers. Fame for that place, from
ships and brave men—such was the prayer   10
made, arms outstretched, at the altar of Hellenic
Zeus by Endaïs' fair sons   Peleus and Telamon
   and by the mighty lord Phokos,

ep. born to the Nereid, Psammathē, at the sea's edge. I
scruple to tell the great deed, both   the killing of Phokos
   just and unjust, that later was
risked and achieved, and how they departed from   15
   this famous isle, which power
drove such brave men from Oinona—I shall stand   Oinona=Aigina
   mute! Not always does
blunt truth uncover her face to advantage;
   silence is sometimes a
man's wisest mode. But

2. if it be bliss, strength of hand, or
   iron-clad war that is
chosen for praise, dig me a trench!   20
   My knees are nimble—
eagles can vault the broad sea. Muses in
chorus most fair once sang for these
men on Pelion's height, while in their midst   men=Aiakids
Apollo put plectrum of gold to his
seven-tongued lyre, leading their

every strain. First they hymned Zeus, then   25
   Thetis, then Peleus,
telling how pampered Hippolyta   after Phokos' death Peleus took
   tried to destroy him through   refuge in Magnesia
devious plots with her lord, Magnesia's
king, as accomplice. She built up a
fabric of lies—that he, their guest, had come to the
nuptial couch of Akastos, to   30
   make an attempt on the

ep. wife of his host. The reverse was the truth! She had
begged him with many sly pleas but,
    angered by speech so perverse, he had
spurned her, fearing the wrath of the god of
    guests. Watching from heaven,
Zeus, the cloud-driving king of immortals, then
    promised that this man should
take as his bride one of the sea-spawned   35
gold-spindled Nereids.   Thetis
    He would persuade her

3. suitor, Poseidon, who frequently   cf. I. 8.27–30
    visits the Dorian   the Isthmian games were Zeus' bribe
isthmus where jubilant crowds, the
    wailing of pipes, and the
strife of strong limbs greet him as god. Ancestral
fate determines all deeds. O Euthymenes,   40
going from Aigina, you sank twice into   maternal uncle
victory's arms, to be touched by the
    music of elegant praise!

Pytheas, this uncle follows your
    path as he glorifies Peleus'
race! Nemea claims him, as does the
    month of Apollo, for he did   when local games were held
trounce every boy who opposed him, here or at   45
Megara. I am rejoiced that the
whole city strives for ends that are noble. Remember—
your toil now finds this sweet answer
    thanks to Menander's high   trainer

ep. fortune! It's right that a builder of athletes should
hail from the city of Athens. But   50
    if you have come here to sing of
Themistios, shout, don't stint! Spread your full   mother's father
    sail at the masthead!

Greet him as boxer and pankratist, tell of his
    two Epidaurian
triumphs, then—guided by fair-haired Graces—
carry these flowery crowns out to the
    forecourt of Aiakos!   Aiakos had a shrine in the city

NEMEAN 6   Achilles and Memnon

For Alkimidas of Aigina, of the Bassid tribe, victor in boys' wrestling, re-
stricted at Nemea to those under fifteen years. This family has produced
successful athletes only in alternate generations; Alkimidas brings his
victory to a father who has no athletic fame, and in the same way his
grandfather, Praxidamas (lines 16–24), brought the first Olympic crown
to be won by an Aiginetan to his father, Sokleides (line 20), a man whose
reputation depended on that of his sons.

Kallias (line 35) and Kreontidas (line 40) are perhaps brothers of
Praxidamas. Alkimidas and a cousin (or perhaps a friend), Polytimidas,
have also competed at Olympia, where boy contenders could be as old as
seventeen, but these two, according to lines 61–3, were assigned impos-
sible opponents.

For other references to Memnon (lines 50–53), see Nemean 3.61–3,
Isthmian 5.40–1, and Isthmian 8.54.
460 BC

1. One is the race of men and of gods! Both take
breath from one mother, though powers distinct   mother=Earth (Gē)
keep us apart, for men are as naught while the
    bronze throne of heaven
rests safe forever. True, we may sometimes resemble the
deathless in grandeur of mind or of body but   5
we cannot know, by day or by night,
what course destiny
marks out and sets for our running.

This Alkimidas proves: that inherited strength,
like to a fruit-bearing field, sometimes
sends up rich nurture for men, then in turn stops,   10
    resting and hoarding its
forces. He comes from the Nemean strife that he loves, a
boy tried in contest who now, having followed this

Zeus-made decree, makes his appearance,
not as a hunter of
glory deprived of his prey, but

ep. fitting his foot to the tracks of his father's own   15
sire, Praxidamas, who was the
first to return to the Aiakids bringing them
garlands from Alpheos as an Olympian victor!
Five times crowned at the Isthmos, at Nemea thrice,
he put an end to Sokleides' obscurity, raising him highest   20
among the offspring of
Hagesimachos, for his three

2. prizewinning sons had all tasted of athletic
toil, then scaled virtue's peak. By god's will, on
no other house in all Greece did the boxer's art   25
    shine with such brilliance—his
halls stored a treasure of victory crowns! I trust this
boast to strike home like an arrow loosed from the
bow. O Muse, send forth a
glory-filled windblast of
words, for while men disappear

stories and songs revive noble deeds, nor is the   30
line of the Bassids lacking in legend!
An ancient race, sailing alone, they carry a
    cargo of praise-themes,
supplying Pieria's ploughmen with many a hymn.
One of them, Kallias, first binding thongs to his
fists, was victor in Pytho's domain,   35
favorite choice of the
nurselings of gold-spindled Leto.   Apollo and Artemis

ep. There at Kastalia he blazed in the night amid
shouts from the Graces; so too the
bridge of the tireless sea praised Kreontidas   bridge=the Isthmos
when, at the third-year killing of bulls by men who   41
live near the shrine of Poseidon, the crown made of

parsley (the lion's herb) covered his
conqueror's brow, under the shadowy
age-old mountains of Phleios.

3. Broad highways open in every direction for   45
those who use tales to embellish this isle, for
Aiakids, ever displaying brave actions,
   give them an outstanding task.
Their name soars high above earth and sea,
leaping as far as the Ethiope land when
Memnon failed to return—heavy the   50
strife that fell upon
him when Achilles leapt from his

car and using the point of his angry spear
stripped that son of bright Eos! Poets of
old discovered this path and, strong in my
   purpose, I shall now
follow. The wave that breaks close to the rigging gives   55
pain to all hearts, so men say. I come, a glad
herald, my willing back bearing a
doubled load as I   praise owed to both victor and ancestors
voice this twenty-fifth boast that

ep. you, o Alkimidas, bring from the contests called
sacred, enriching your glorious   60
clan. At the precinct of Zeus it was only the
lot's early fall that robbed you, my boy—Polytimidas
too—of a pair of Olympian garlands!
To a swift dolphin that cuts through the sea I would
liken Melesias, driver who   trainer, cf. O. 8.54, N. 4.93
guides your skill and your strength.

For Sogenes of Aigina, the late-born son of Thearion (lines 8, 58) of the
Euxenid tribe, victor in the boys' pentathlon, which consisted of running,
jumping, javelin throw, discus cast, and wrestling, the last of which could
be avoided with wins in the first four (cf. lines 70–3).

Because of his legendary violence after the fall of Troy, Achilles' son,
Neoptolemos, was an unusual choice as mythic subject (lines 102–5), but
he appears here as the last of the Aiakid heroes, a son who completed the
work of his father.

In its course, the ode marks a kind of coming of age for Sogenes as it
moves from the realm of the birth goddess Eleithyia (line 1) to that of the
patron of young warriors, Herakles (line 86).
485 BC ?

1. Birth Goddess, throne-mate of deep-purposed Moirai,
daughter of powerful Hera, listen, o
   maker of children! Without you,
no one sees light and the kindly dark,
or takes his portion of youth from Hebē, your
bright-limbed sister, though we do not draw that first breath as   5
equals, for each one is yoked to his separate fate.
Marked by pentathlon success, thanks to you,   <small>you=Eleithyia</small>
Sogenes, son of Thearion, must now be sung!

His is a song-loving city, the home-place of
Aiakid heroes—spearmen ready to   10
   honor a temper tested by strife.
When a man acts and succeeds, he
casts a sweet song-subject into the streams of the
Muses, but even magnificent boldness is shadowed,
if praise fail! Noble deeds we can mirror only when
garlanded Memory aids us in making a   15
chanted fame-bearing song—repayment for toil.

ep. Sages whose wits are not dulled by greed
know the third wind in its coming. Rich men and   third wind=storm
paupers alike all move toward the tomb.
I am convinced that the tale of Odysseus,   20
rendered in Homer's honey-sweet words,
    outruns his deeds—a

2. tissue of lies and winged devices
lends him a grandeur of sorts, for poetical
    tales can lead us astray.
Men in a mob have hearts that are blind;
could they see truth, strong Ajax would never have   25
thrust a pale blade through his lungs, raging because of the
armor, for after Achilles, he was the best of
all of the warriors sent by the favoring breezes of
Zephyr to Troy, to bring back the wife of the

fair Menelaos. But Hades' sea-surge will   30
break over all, whether seeing or blind, while
    honor waits only where god
nurtures the fame of the dead. As an
ally he came to the navel of deep-wombed earth—   Delphi
he, Neoptolemos, now lies in Pythian soil!—
after he'd sacked Priam's city where Danaans   35
suffered as well. Sailing home, he missed Skyros,
wandered, and finally touched on the Epirote shore.

ep. Briefly he ruled as Molossian king—
office yet held by his line—then with riches
taken as booty from Troy he set out to   40
visit the god and there, quarrelling over   god=Apollo
sacrificed meats, a man with a
    knife cut him down.

3. His Delphic hosts felt deep grief, but such was
destiny's claim. An Aiakid lord was to
    rest for all time in the most ancient
grove of the god, close by the walls of the   45

temple, a guardian presence when men bearing
sacrifice came in their hero-processions. For justice,
three words suffice: not false is the witness marking the
brave deeds of sons sprung from you, o   sons=Aiakids
Aigina, and from great Zeus! This I declare: a   50

highroad of tales stretches forth from that house,
marked by their luminous actions. Still,
    respite is sweet while, even in
honey or petal-soft pleasures of love,
surfeit may hide. We differ each in our inborn
strengths—some take this as their portion, some that, and   55
no one is everywhere fortunate. Not one can I
name to whom Moira has brought success that is
fixed, yet to you, o Thearion, she offers

ep. suitable wealth, nor does she rob you of
sense as you cultivate boldness in action!   60
I am a guest; scorning dark blame I
bring my friend genuine glory—praise like
free-flowing water, the wage that is owed to
    men of nobility.

4. Here present, the man from Achaia whose   a guest from Epiros?
hall overlooks the Ionian sea will not   65
    fault me—I trust in guest-friendship—while
citizen eyes I meet with pride for,
clearing my path of all violence, I
don't overshoot. May the future be kind! One who
listens can tell if I sing out of tune or whisper lies.
Euxenid Sogenes, hear my sworn oath!   70
I have not stepped to the mark to give my swift

tongue the spear-cast that sends a man out of the
ring, no sweat on his neck, limbs not yet   I haven't begun so well that
    touched by the sun! But if there was   I can stop here
toil, the following joy is the greater.
Let be! Though roused to a loud shout,   75
I won't be rough as I pay off my debt to this victor.

Crowns are simple to weave, so begin—the
Muse will join gold with pale ivory, adding the
lily-like bloom that she draws from the foam of the sea!   coral

ep. Sound Zeus' name, then whirl out a storm of   80
many-voiced Nemean hymns—but gently! On
this sacred ground one hails the gods' king with
sounds that are suave, for he begat Aiakos
here, so men say, his seed well received by the
      mother, making a   mother=Aigina

5. founder of cities for my famous land and for   founder=Aiakos
you, Herakles, a benevolent brother and   86
      friend! I believe that firm love from a
neighbor brings joy beyond price to a
man with a relish for company. Should this hold
true among gods then, trusting in you, o
tamer of giants, and nursing a tender concern for his   90
father, Sogenes may without fear dwell in the
street of his forebears where he has a hall

placed as if yoked to a double pair, with
precincts of yours to his right and his left,
      as he goes forth. O blessed one,   94
you have the power to bend Hera's lord   Zeus
or the maid with grey eyes, while often you   Athena
strengthen a man when there seems no salvation! Match his
youth and his lustrous old age to a steady life-force,
weaving for him a long fabric of
happiness, and may his sons' sons ever keep,   100

ep. even surpass this present honor! I have not
dragged Neoptolemos into my song with rough
words—this my heart denies! But cutting the
same furrow three or four times ends in futility,
just like the child who barks out to the others,
      "Korinth was son of Zeus!"   cry from a children's game,
                                                                       answered by an attack

NEMEAN 8   Ajax in Death and in Battle

For Deinias of Aigina, of the Chariad tribe, and for his father, Megas, now dead (lines 16, 44–7). As winner of the double-course footrace (about 400 yards), the newly adolescent boy (lines 1–5) has repeated an earlier triumph of his father, but the theme of envy so strongly present in the ode suggests that, in his own lifetime, Megas was not given the praise that was due to him.

In its mythic section, the song returns to Ajax the honor denied to him after the death of Achilles, when the Greek army refused to grant him that hero's arms and he killed himself (line 25–7; cf. Nemean 7.24– 30 and Isthmian 4.35–9). For the birth of Ajax, see Isthmian 6. Ca. 460 BC

1. Hora, mistress of love's holy sweets,   goddess of ripe youth
    Kyprian herald
thronèd upon eyelids of boys and girls, one
suitor you gently raise up, another you
        treat in the opposite fashion!
Best pleasure comes when a timely choice,
made among noble desires, takes its prize.   5

Such loves, shepherds of Kypris' own gifts,   Aphrodite
    served at the couch where
Zeus lay with Aigina, whence came a son, a   Aiakos
king for Oinona, finest in counsel and might.   the island of Aigina
    Many men begged, and often, to
enter his presence when, uncalled, the flower of
bravery chose to obey his command—   10

ep. heroes who marshalled the forces of rock-bound
Athens and Pelopids dwelling in Sparta.
Like them a suppliant, I would touch
    Aiakos' sacred knees in behalf of the

142

townsmen and city he loved, bringing a
Lydian crown that is inlaid with music, the   15
badge of the double-course Nemean race
    where, like Megas, his father,
Deinias triumphed. Bliss planted by god stops
    longest with men—bliss like the

2. wealth that once rested on Kinyras   favorite of Apollo and Aphrodite
    out on the Kyprian isle.
Light feet at a standstill, I take breath, then speak!
Tales are told and retold but a newfound invention,   20
    put to the test, is at risk.
Fame is a feast for the envious who,
leaving the lesser, devour what is fine.

Such envy bit into Telamon's son,   Ajax
    thrusting him onto his
sword. Bold at heart, the man of no words
loses his match with oblivion while a   25
    slippery lie takes the prize.
Secret Greek ballots favored Odysseus;
Ajax, the gold armor lost, wrestled with gore.

ep. Unequal too were the wounds cut by their
spears in warm enemy flesh as, under attack, they
sheltered the newly killed corpse of Achilles, or   30
    labored through other slaughter-filled days.
Yes, loathsome slander existed of old,
companion and ally of crafty suggestions,
ready with schemes and injurious
    taunts! It violates all that is
bright but fosters a decadent fame where
    no worthy deeds can be shown.

3. O father Zeus, let such practices   35
    never be mine! Let me
follow straight paths and leave, when I die, no evil
fame to my sons! Some pray for gold, some for vast

lands, but I hope to gladden the
city, then bury these limbs, having praised what is
worthy and blamed the doers of wrong.

Excellence grows like the trunk of a tree   40
    under fresh dew; it is
raised to the sky's liquid heights by men who love
justice and song. Friends fill various needs;
    they are best among troubles, but
joy, too, would offer its truth to the
eyes of another. Megas, to bring back your

ep. life—this I cannot do (empty hopes   45
end in collapse) but for Chariads and for your homeland
I can erect a Muse-stone that shouts out the
    doubled triumphs of two pairs of feet!
I shall joyously cast a fit boast toward your
deed, for with magical chants one may deaden the
pain of hard toil. Ancient indeed is the   50
    victory hymn—it was born   cf. line 31
even before the strife of Adrastos with
men of the city of Kadmos.   when the Nemean games were founded

NEMEAN 9 Amphiaraos Is Rescued from Shame

For Chromios, son of Hagesidamos and, as first among Hieron's associates, regent of Aitna (line 2, cf. Nemean 1). The battle of Heloros, 492 BC (referred to in line 39), was one in which Chromios had supported Hieron's predecessor and older brother, Gelo, when he conquered Syracuse and established the Deinomenids as the most powerful family in Sicily. Chromios has been victor in a chariot race held not at Nemea but perhaps at Sikyon, where the games for Apollo reputedly were founded by Adrastos while that Argive leader was in exile, before the first expedition against Thebes (lines 1, 9–11, 53, and cf. Nemean 10.28). For other episodes from the Argive expeditions against Thebes, see Olympian 6.13–7 and Pythian 8.39–55.

474 BC ?

1. Muses, we'll dance from Apollo at Sikyon
back to the new-built city of Aitna where
    guests are besieging the
wide-open doors of Chromios' opulent house!
    Strike up a hymn made sweet with words!
Mounting his car with its winning team, he
    signals a chant for the mother and twins   Leto, with Apollo and Artemis
who serve as guardians on Pytho's steep slope.   5

2. Men say a deed nobly done should never be
buried in silence. Song is required, filled with
    sacred acclaim, so let's
waken the vibrating lyre and the pipe for this
    finest equestrian contest
held for Apollo by Asopos' streams, as   river near Sikyon
    long ago set by Adrastos. Remembering this,
I shall now armor that hero in praise.   10

3. As king of that land, he founded new festivals,   the region of Asopos
trials of man's muscle and strife of bright cars to
    prove the great fame of his
city. Abandoning Argos and ancestral halls, he had
    fled civil war and the schemings of
Amphiaraos when, bested by force, the
    sons of Talaos no longer held power. A   sons=Adrastos and brothers
stronger man silences what once was just.   15

4. Then, by sending Eriphylē, tamer of men, to their
rival as wife and true pledge, he and his brothers
    made themselves lords of the
fair-haired Danaans. They marshalled a host against seven-gate
    Thebes, but their path was not marked by
favoring birds, nor did the Kronian
    fire-bolt encourage their unthinking move but
marked it instead as a path to avoid.   20

5. Ruin was plain but the host rushed upon it
armored in bronze, horses in panoply, only to
    bury all hope of return
there on the banks of Ismenos when white
    petals of smoke fed on their limbs.
Seven pyres swallowed their youthful remains, but
    Zeus, for Amphiaraos, split earth's broad
breast with his bolt and hid hero and team,   25

6. lest Periklymenos' lance should lodge in his
back to shame that brave heart. Caught by
    fear sent from heaven,
even the sons of the gods flee. Kronian one,
    if this might be, I would postpone to the
edges of Time any life-and-death
    battle with spearmen of Carthage. I ask
orderly peace for the children of Aitna—   30

7. o father Zeus, unite them in citywide
festivals! These are horse-loving men,

their spirits stronger than
wealth's lure. Hard to believe?—yes, for so often the
   reverent Shame that brings fair renown is   *aidos*, sense of duty
stolen by greed. Still, had you borne Chromios'
   shield, mounted, on foot, or at sea, you'd
know how that goddess, in times of sharp peril,   35

8. readied his militant heart to stave off the
havoc of Ares. Only a few can
   urge the repulse of a
blood-filled cloud, sending it back upon enemy
   lines, though Hektor, it's said,
bloomed with such glory by Skamander's streams, and the
   same light, on the banks of Heloros   Battle of Heloros, 492 BC
near to the place men call Areia's ford,   40

9. shone on the son of Hagesidamos,
yet in his earliest manhood. His many
   later deeds, done in the
dust of dry land or on the neighboring sea,
   I shall recount at some other time.
Youthful trials, undertaken with justice,
   lead to a gentle old age. May he know his
portion of bliss as a gift from the gods!   45

10. If, with much wealth, a man conquers fame, his
two mortal feet can try no higher summit.
   Peaceful contentment   Hesychia, cf. O. 4.16, P. 8.1
loves the symposium; victory blooms there afresh in
   elegant song as, close to the
mixing bowl, voices grow confident.
   Pour in the wine, sweet prophet of
revelry—stir it and serve up the lusty   50

11. child of the vine in the silver cups taken by
Chromios' mares and brought, with crowns formally
   plaited for Leto's fair son,   Apollo

from sacred Sikyon! Zeus, father of all, I
   ask that the Graces may join me in
singing this triumph—let me surpass many
   rivals as I give praise, casting my
song-spear nearest of all to the mark of the Muses!   55

For Theaios of Argos, son of Oulias (line 23), apparently in celebration of
a double victory taken not at Nemea but at the Hekatombaia, the Argive
festival for Hera (line 21). A frequent victor in wrestling—three times
each at Nemea and Isthmia and once at Delphi (lines 27–9)—Theaios
hopes for a crown from Olympia (lines 29–30), and this ambition is re-
flected in the song's unparalleled focus on a gracious Zeus; all the
mythic figures mentioned are descendants of his.
Date unknown.

1. Sing, Graces, of Danaos' city where his fifty
    daughters sit their bright thrones—give praise to
Argos, the homeland of Hera, meet for a god and
    blazing with ten-thousand
daring adventures! Perseus' pursuit of the
Gorgon Medusa makes a long tale, and
many a city of Egypt was   5
    founded by Epaphos' skills, nor   child of Zeus and Io, an Argive priestess
was Hypermnestra astray when she kept her   the one Danaid who did
    sword's single vote in its sheath!   not kill her husband

To Diomedes grey-eyed Athena long ago   leader of Argives at Troy
    gave immortality; Theban earth
rescued the Oikleid prophet, storm-cloud of war but   Amphiaraos
    slashed by the fire-bolts of
Zeus, and for beautiful women Argos was
foremost—Alkmena's bed and Danaë's   10
couch were both of them known to Zeus!
    Justice and ripe thought he
joined in Lynkeus and in Adrastos' old   early kings of Argos
    father; he nourished Amphitryon's

149

ep. spear, then made him his kin—happiest state—
after that bronze-armored warrior had conquered the
Teleboiai. He, the monarch of heaven, entered the   15
hall of that hero, dressed in his likeness, but
bearing the intrepid seed that made Herakles, whose bride,
Hebē most fair, strolls on Olympos close to her mother,   cf. N. 1.71–2;
    goddess of marriage fulfilled.   I. 4.59–60

2. Too short is my tongue to relate all the splendors
    known to the precinct at Argos—
surfeit is ever a burden. Yet we must waken the   20
    strings of the lyre and
think upon wrestling. Hera's bronze prize calls
men to the slaughter of oxen and to her
games, where Theaios, Oulias' son,
    twice was victorious,
winning the right to forget his
    well-endured labors. He had

already routed a host of Greek rivals at Pytho; with   Delphi
    fortune beside him, he'd taken
garlands at Nemea and at the Isthmos, clearing a   26
    field for the Muses' plough—
winner three times where the sea-gates stand,   the Isthmos
thrice on the ground that Adrastos made sacred!   Nemea
But, father Zeus, what his mind most desires his
    tongue treats with silence. All
ends lie with you but he, from a heart not untried,   30
    begs a return for his courage.

ep. This that I sing is a plea known to the god and to
all who would strive at the summit of athletic contests,
that peak guarded by Pisa and Herakles' games.   Olympia
As sacred prelude, sweet Attic voices have circled him
twice and the fruit of the olive has   35
journeyed to Hera's brave people in jars of fired earth
    covered with painted designs.   Panathenaic amphoras

3. Often have men of your mother's line known
    victory honors, Theaios,
thanks to the Graces and to the Tyndarid sons of the   Kastor and Pollux
    swan. Were I kin to   Zeus came to Leda as a swan
Thrasykles or to Antaias, I would not   maternal ancestors
lower my gaze here in Agos. So many   40
times did this horse-rearing town of Proïtos   early Argive king
    blossom with wreaths brought from
Korinth by this pair, and think of the four
    won among men at Kleonai!   Nemea

They came from Sikyon silvered with wine cups, from
    Pellana mantled in soft woollen
cloaks, while their myriad bronzes cannot be numbered—
    time is too short—
offered as prizes at Kleitor, at Tegea,   45
and in the high-perched towns of Achaia, or
shown near the racecourse of Lykaian
    Zeus as objects of strife to be
taken by men whose strong hands or feet
    make them victorious.

ep. Kastor, we know, came with Pollux, his brother to
visit Pamphaes, so no one can marvel that athletic   victor's ancestor
skill resides in this stock. Those two, with Hermes and
Herakles, watch over flourishing contests at
Sparta, city of broad dancing places.
They care for men of right justice and surely the
    offspring of gods may be trusted.

4. Changing by turns they pass one day with Zeus, their dear   55
    father, the next hidden deep in the
caves that lie under Therapna, sharing an equal fate.
    This was the portion—
rather than dwelling forever on high as a
god—that Pollux had chosen when
Kastor lay dying. Angered somehow,
    during a quarrel about

cattle, Idas had wounded him,   60
    using the point of his spear.   Idas and Lynkeus are cousins of Kastor and Pollux

Where he kept watch, high on Taÿgetos,
    Lynkeus, most sharp-eyed of mortals, had
spotted the pair where they sat on a fallen oak tree.   pair=Kastor and Pollux
    He and Idas, his
brother, attacked at a run, meaning great
harm, but by Zeus' contrivance they
suffered instead a most fearsome   65
    end, for the child born of Leda   child=Pollux
followed and caught them
    standing at their father's tomb. They

ep. wrenched up the polished gravestone to aim it at
Pollux, but he did not fall, nor were his ribs crushed.
Lunging, he thrust the swift tip of his spear into Lynkeus'
lungs while Zeus, with his smoldering bolt, shattered   70
Idas. The two burned untended in
that desert place: strife with the
    stronger is hard to maintain.

5. Pollux the Tyndarid ran back to Kastor, his
    once mighty brother, whom he dis-
covered, not dead but trembling and gasping for
    breath. Groaning aloud and
shedding hot tears he cried, "Kronian father,   75
what can release me from grief such as this?
Lord, let me die with him, here!
    Honor departs when a man is
shorn of his kin, for those friends are
    few who will help with his burden."

Such was his cry and Zeus at once faced him,
    answering, "You are my son.
That one was later begat by the husband and hero who   Tyndareus
    lay with your mother
planting his mortal seed in her womb. But come—I   81

grant you this choice. If, for your own part,
turning from death and hateful old age
    you would live throughout time with
me on Olympos, close to Athena and
      Ares the black-speared,

ep. that same lot may be yours. Or if instead   85
you choose to strive for your brother and share with him equally,
you may for half of your time take breath in the underworld
then, for the other, in heaven's gold halls."
Pollux knew no indecision;
he first opened the eyes, then set free the voice of
    Kastor, the bronze-belted warrior.

NEMEAN 11   The City's Hearth

For Aristagoras of Tenedos, an island just off the coast of Turkey.
Aristagoras has been successful in local athletic competitions (lines 19–
21), but the occasion of this song is his installation as a member of the lo-
cal ruling council. The meeting place of such groups was thought of as
the dining hall or hearth of the city; visitors were received there, and it
was sacred to Hestia, the hearth goddess. Zeus Xenios (line 8) watches
over strangers and guards the laws of hospitality.
Date unknown but probably post–450 BC

1. Daughter of Rhea, Hestia, mistress of all civic hearths,
sister of Zeus all-supreme and of Hera, his throne-mate,
take Aristagoras into your hall! Bring him close to your
glorious scepter, with his companions—men who in
service to you keep Tenedos firm and upright,   5

offering smoke and many libations to you as
first of divinities. Voices and lyre-tones sound while the
law of Zeus Xenios rules at tables of unbroken
feasting. May he finish his twelve months of
office heart-whole and in high repute!   10

ep. This man I hail as blessed, first in his father, Arkesilas,
then in his form and inherited boldness. Still,
be a man rich, surpassing in beauty,
his strength supreme in athletic games, even he must remember that
his mortal limbs, today wrapped in splendor   15
will, when the end comes, wear earth.

2. Townsmen will offer fine words of praise, while melodies
throbbing with sweetness adorn him, for victories—
sixteen in number, won among neighboring rivals in

wrestling and much-vaunted pankratic strife—now   20
garland his glorious race and crown Aristagoras.

The hesitant hopes of his parents kept the boy's strength from contests at
Pytho and trials at Olympia, but to this I will
swear: had he entered the games at Kastalia or those near the
shady Kronian hill, he would have made a more   25
noble return than any opponent! After the fourth-year

ep. contest of Herakles, he would have danced, binding dark
olive-twigs into his hair! But among mortals
one is cast down from success by a
mindless ambition, another, doubting too much of his   30
strength, misses his proper good fortune, his hand
checked by a heart that lacks boldness.

3. Easy it is to infer that this is the blood of Pisandros,
Spartan of old who came with Orestes, leading an army of
bronze-clad Aiolian men from Amyklai—blood mixed   35
through Melanippos, the mother's forebear, with the
streams of Ismenos. But archaic virtues   river of Thebes

ever yield varying strengths as one generation follows the
last. The dark fields of earth do not send up a regular crop,
nor, as the years turn, do fruit-trees bear scented blossoms   40
of equal richness, but only in alternate seasons.
So is the course of mortality shaped by

ep. Moira. A clear sign from Zeus of what he intends comes to   Fate
no man, and yet we embark upon dangerous courses,
eager for countless deeds, limbs obedient to impious   45
hopes while forethought dissolves in the distance.
As he gains profit, a man should seek measure; a passion for
what can't be reached is madness too sharp.

ISTHMIAN 1   A Hymn for Kastor and Iolaos

For Herodotos of Thebes, victor in the chariot race. This is the sixth Isthmian chariot crown to be won by a Theban (lines 10–11), and Herodotos—who drives his own chariot (line 15)—has already won in many lesser contests (lines 56–9). The closing lines ask for future victories at Delphi and Olympia (lines 64–6).

The victor's father, Asopodoros, had at one time taken refuge at Orchomenos but has since been allowed to return to Thebes (lines 35–40); he may have been the city's cavalry commander at the battle at Plataia (479 BC), sent into temporary exile when the Persians withdrew from Greece (Herodotos 9.69).

The opening lines assert that the poet, in order to honor this Theban occasion, has set aside a commission from Keos for a paean to be performed at Delos.

446 BC ?

1. Theba, my mother, you of the golden shield,
your need comes first, though time is lacking!
May rocky Delos, where I am promised,
be without anger—among good men,
what is more dear than a parent?   5
Yield, o isle of Apollo! With god's aid I shall
   yoke the two tasks in a single fulfillment,

dancing for long-haired Phoibos with sailors from
wave-washed Keos and praising the
Isthmian spur, fence of the sea, for the
six contest crowns that were there granted to   10
Kadmeian men—triumphant   Thebans
fame for the land where Alkmena gave
   birth to a child without fear who   Herakles

ep. terrified Geryon's angry hounds. I mean to   Tenth Labor
fashion a prize for Herodotos, chariot-

156

driver who does not abandon the
reins to another, and I would harness him now to the   15
Kastor strain, or to the Iolaion. Those two   traditional melodic forms
bravest of heroes, one born in Thebes, one in   Iolaos, nephew of Herakles
   Lakedaimon, though prime   Kastor, Pollux's brother

2. chariot men, tried games of all sorts and took
tripods, vases, and wine cups of
gold to furbish their halls—such was their   20
taste for victory garlands! Their
spirit burned clear when they raced in the
stadium, naked or carrying loud-clashing
   shields—how it sparkled when

javelins leapt from their hands, or when they
hurled the stone discus! Not yet was the   25
pentathlon held, but a separate crown was
set for each contest. Often did
these two appear, twigs bound
thick in their hair, close beside Dirka's streams   at Thebes
   or where Eurotas flows, for   at Sparta

ep. Iphikles' son was by blood of the Spartoi while   Iolaos
Kastor, a Tyndarid, held a high seat at Therapna   hill near Sparta
   dwelling among the Achaians. Greetings!
I shall mantle Poseidon, his sacred Isthmos and
Onchestos' shore with my song, while I honor this
man and give voice to the glorious fate of his
   father, Asopodoros,

3. welcomed at Orchomenos by ancestral fields when   35
shipwreck and freezing disaster had
cast him ashore, badly battered,
out of the measureless sea. Now the fixed
fate of his fathers sets him once
more on a fair-weather course! He who has   40
   toiled gains prudence of mind;

if to high deeds he brings passion as well,
working and spending, then all men must
search out brave boasts, praising from ungrudging
hearts when he succeeds. This, for a
man skilled in song, is a light task—to   45
speak a fair word as payment for labor,
    sounding it out for all to enjoy.

ep. Wages are sweet, though they vary for various
tasks, for whether a man be shepherd or farmer,
    fowler, or fed by the sea, he would
ever defend his own belly from harsh pangs of hunger. Still,
he who takes much-desired glory from battle or games   50
gets highest pay— praise that blossoms from
    tongues of strangers and friends.

4. Our praise is owed to the master of earthquakes, Poseidon
Kronos' son, neighbor, and patron of
chariot racing, and we must add a loud
shout for your sons, Amphitryon,   *Herakles and Iphikles*
naming, among circling courses,   56
Demeter's famed grove at Eleusis, the valley of
    Minyas, and also Euboia.

Protesilas, to these I would add your   *Theban hero, honored with games*
shrine at Phylakē among the Achaians,   *at the Gulf of Pagasai*
but to tell all that the games-master, Hermes,   60
gave to Herodotos and to his team—
this the short length of my song will
never permit. What rests in silence
    often brings greater delight.

ep. Lifted on high by the luminous wings of
singing Pierian Muses, let him take garlands from   65
    Pytho and Elis to bind on his hand,   *Delphi and Olympia*
fixing the fame of seven-gate Thebes! He who buries his
riches indoors while he sneers at outsiders
fails to consider the soul he will render,
    naked of glory, to Hades.

ISTHMIAN 2   Money and the Muse

For Xenokrates of Akragas, in Sicily, brother of Theron, the city's ruler. At some unknown date Xenokrates, who is now dead, took this victory with a chariot driven, exceptionally, by another nobleman, the Nikomachos of lines 22–8. Like Pythian 6, an earlier ode for Xenokrates, this song addresses the victor's son, Thrasyboulos, who probably commissioned it. The tone of friendly irony ("there was a time when I praised you without being paid") reflects Pindar's long acquaintance with this nephew of Theron; an early drinking song was addressed to him (fr. 124a.b SM), and here Nikasippos, the messenger who brings Pindar's script and performance notes, is directed to a "much honored comrade and host" (lines 47–8).
Ca. 470 BC

1. Men of an earlier time, o Thrasyboulos,
    mounted the car of the gold-crowned
Muses and, finding a glorious lyre there,
    lightly aimed arrows of
honeyed boy-praise at
any fair youth who showed the sweet
ripeness that courts Aphrodite.   5

The Muse of those days was not whorish and profit-mad,
    nor were her whispering songs,
faces bedizened with silver, put up for
    sale by a sweet-tongued
Terpsichora—
she who now bids us to follow that
truth-telling phrase of the Argive: 10

ep. "Money! It's money that makes the man!"
    spoken by one who lost riches, then friends.
You understand. Not unknown is the

Isthmian chariot crown that I sing,
one that Poseidon
gave to Xenokrates, sending a garland of   15
Dorian parsley to bind in his hair—an

2. honor for him who was master of chariots and
    beacon for men of Akragas.
Marked at Krisa by mighty Apollo he   cf. P. 6
    gained glory there, and while
taking Erechtheid
prizes in luminous Athens   20
he could not fault the sure, saving

hand of Nikomachos, driver who knew when to
    loosen the reins. When he appeared,   he=Nikomachos
truce-bearing Elian heralds of Zeus, once his
    satisfied guests,
recognized him
and, as he sank upon Victory's knees,   25
gave him sweet welcome, there in their

ep. homeland, that precinct men know as the
    grove of Olympian Zeus, where the sons of
Ainesidamos were joined with an   father of Theron and Xenokrates
undying fame. O Thrasyboulos, your father's
halls are in truth   30
not without knowledge of pleasure-filled
revels and honey-sweet songs of acclaim!

2. No hill obstructs, nor is the path steep when
    honors from Helikon's maids are
carried to men of repute. My discus is thrown;
    now let the cast of my
spear outdistance all others in   35
length, as did Xenokrates'
temper in sweetness! Modest in

converse with townsmen, a Hellene when training a
   horse, he embraced all feasts of the gods,
nor did any ill-wind ever cause him to
   take in his sails at a
table readied for guests—   40
his port was Phasis in summer, in
winter the mouth of the Nile.   furthest points to east and south

ep. Since all minds are swathed in envious
   hopes, the deeds of a father must never be
silenced. Nor should this song meet
any such end! I did not make it for   45
idle repose,
so, Nikasippos, distribute these words when you   organize a performance
come to my much honored comrade and friend!

For Melissos of Thebes, son of Telesiades of the Kleonomid tribe, and victor at the Isthmos in the pankration (line 62), at Nemea in the horse race (line 13). Melissos is evidently still quite young, for crowns taken among local boys are mentioned (line 89), as is the name of his trainer, Orseas (90–91); perhaps his youth allowed him to be his own jockey.

Reported by ancient editors as coming from two separate odes, these lines are generally now taken to be parts of a single song, with a triad missing between lines 18 and 19. Some scholars have supposed that the opening was in fact a later addition, composed on the occasion of a second victory taken by Melissos.

474/3 BC ?

1. Should a man prosper in power of wealth or
glory of contest, yet limit his excess,
he deserves praise from his city. Zeus,
you are the source of
men's splendid deeds, but bliss abides longer where   5
    reverence is—
brief is its flowering if minds are bent.

We must repay with our songs a noble man's
glorious deeds—he should revel to elegant
hymns! Such is the fate of Melissos, whose heart
now turns toward mirth,   10
crowned in twin contests, first in the Isthmian glen,
    then in the vale of the   Nemea
deep-chested lion when heralds named Thebē   local nymph of Thebes

ep. after he'd won in the hippodrome. His
ancestors' prowess he does not betray.
You know the fame that Kleonymos long ago   founder of victor's clan
won with his chariots, and think of his mother's line,   16

Laios' descendants, exhausting their wealth in
contests of four-horse teams!
Life shifts this way and that as the days turn—
only the race of the gods goes unscarred.
                    [end of Isthmian 3]

2. Thanks to the gods, o Melissos, you opened the
way at the Isthmos, giving me myriad   20
paths for a song that pursues splendid triumphs
such as Kleonomids
ever display, as with god's aid they journey toward
    life's mortal end. Shifting winds
now and again rush upon men and drive them along.

Thebans of old honored this tribe as   25
friendly to neighbors and free from clamorous
pride, while those witnessing breezes of fame that
fly from the mouths of
living and dead they feel in full measure.
    Their acts of bravery
stretch to the pillars of Herakles—   30

ep. noble success goes no further! They were
breeders of horses and pleasing to bronze-clad
Ares, but one day of battle's harsh snowstorm
orphaned the family hearth of four men.
Now after months of chill winter darkness the   35
earth shows an intricate
pattern as if, by design of the gods,
deep red roses had come into bloom.

3. He who as earthshaker dwells in Onchestos   Poseidon
and at the sea-bridge near Korinth offers this
excellent hymn to your race to rouse up their
ancient renown   40
gained by glorious deeds but lately
    asleep. Wakened, she
shines like the dawn-star among lesser lights!

She told of chariot victories taken at   she=the ancient renown, line 39
Athens and in the games of Adrastos at
Sikyon, offering songs of that time in   45
garlands like these.
They kept no car from festival contest, but joyously   they=your race, line 41
    spent to rival all
Greece. Silence obscures the untried and,

ep. even for those who make the attempt,
fortune is veiled 'til the end, when her gifts   50
vary in kind. Sometimes the guile, even of
base men, can trip up the stronger. You know the
bloodstained courage of Ajax—how,
late in the night he thrust himself
onto his own gory blade, blamed by
all of the Greeks who had come to Troy.

4. Still, Homer has honored him, using oracular   55
phrases and measured verse to set forth the
whole of his valor for future men's pleasure.
Words spoken well
move like a god's voice and deeds nobly done
    shine over sea and the fruitful
land—a beacon-flame not to be darkened.   60

May friendly Muses help us to kindle a
torch of sung praise, a well-deserved pankratic
crown for Melissos, offspring of Telesiades!
Bold like the bellowing
lion at heart, in guile he's a fox who falls on his   65
    back to check the swoop of an
eagle. Use any trick to extinguish a foe.

ep. He wasn't granted Orion's physique:
not much to look at but hard to support when
he takes the best of a fall! Just such a man   man=Herakles
came to the house of Antaios from Kadmeian   Libyan giant
Thebes—not tall, but unswerving in spirit.   71

He meant to challenge rich
Libya's lord, that visitors' skulls might
no longer roof the shrine of Poseidon, this

5. son of Alkmena! He went to Olympos
after he'd traveled the earth and the cliff-bound
sea, ensuring smooth passage for sailors, and   75
now, most blessed, he
dwells in a golden hall close beside Zeus, honored by
    gods, and takes Hebē as
wife, with Hera his mother-in-law!   cf. Hesiod *Eoiai* fr. 25.26–33

Spreading his feast outside the gate of Elektra
here at a circle of new-built altars, we   80
sacrifice victims for eight bronze-clad dead—
Herakles' sons born to
Kreon's child, Megara. Flames rise as day sinks and
    throughout the night
savory smoke lashes the air. On the

ep. next day our annual games reach their   85
goal, where strength does its work, and where
this man, his head silvered with myrtle,
displayed his two victories, already holding a
third, won among boys while he was yet
under his pilot's experienced hand. I   pilot=trainer
dance for him now, and for Orseas,   91
sprinkling both with joyful rewards!

For Phylakidas of Aigina, son of Lampon, younger brother of Pytheas (cf. Nemean 5), grandson of Kleonikos (his father's father, line 55), and victor in the boys' pankration, for which he has been trained by his brother (line 59). For an earlier victory taken in the same place, see Isthmian 6; evidently, there has also been a pankratic victory at Nemea (lines 18–20).

In a community where many men have recently died in the recent battle at Salamis (lines 47–51), this ode must praise a boy for an athletic success; consequently, it reminds listeners that when the gods judge the inner quality of courage (line 10), visible magnificence is not the determining factor, while the fame that follows such judgments is the same for athletes and for warrior heroes (lines 26–7). The series of questions, at lines 38–42, asks for an unspoken (or perhaps spoken) response from the audience, the answer in every case being "Achilles!"
478 BC ?

1. Theia, many named goddess, mother of Helios,   *divine light / sun*
men, thanks to you, count gold as supreme!
Ships that contend at sea or
horses harnessed to chariots
are through your power discovered, o   5
queen, as marvels engaged in a
    swift-circling strife.

So too with the triumphant athlete, when he gains
glory in contest and crowns, won by hands
or by swift feet, are bound in his
hair. Yet valor is judged by the   10
gods: two things, when joined, nourish a
life in its prime, adding fullness of
    flowering bliss—

ep. good fortune followed by sounding praise.
Seek not to be Zeus! You have all if a
share of such blessings is yours. Mortal ambitions suit   15
men who must die. Isthmia stores up your
twice-blooming glory, Phylakidas, and
Nemea knows of the pankratic crowns
taken by you and by Pytheas! Yet, with
Aiakids absent, my song has no savor. I've   20
come for the two sons of Lampon, bringing the

2. Graces into this well-ordered city. One who has   Charites
taken a clear path of god-sponsored deeds
should never skimp as he mixes due
boasting with music as payment for   25
toil! So warrior heroes are paid—
sung by the lyre and the babbling
    many-voiced pipe

since ages past. Their worship, by Zeus' decree, keeps
poets at work. In Aitolian rites
bright flames of sacrifice honor the   30
powerful Oineidai, and at   Meleagros and Tydeus
Thebes Iolaos the driver is sung,   nephew of Herakles
Perseus in Argos, in Sparta,
    Kastor with Pollux, but

ep. here on Oinona the great-hearted   Oinona=Aigina
spirit of Aiakos' line is supreme.   35
Twice they ravaged the city of Troy, following
Herakles first, then with the Atreids.
Lift me now, well off the ground! Speak out!
Who were the killers of Kyknos? of
Hektor? of Memnon, the unfearing Ethiope   40
chief, armored in bronze? Whose lance, where
Kaïkos flows, wounded brave Telephos?

3. My lips make Aigina, luminous isle, home to these
heroes; their deeds have long towered   these heroes=Aiakids

high in this place! For them　　　　　　　　　　　　　　　45
my practiced tongue keeps many a
shaft while the city of Ajax, now
tested by Ares, asserts that our　　　　　　　　battle of Salamis, 480 BC
　　sailors sustained her—

Salamis!—while during Zeus' thunderous storm
blood came like hail from uncounted men. But　　　　50
drown all such boasting in silence!
Zeus deals out good and bad,
Zeus commands all! Honors
such as today's want a honey-dipped
　　victory shout.

ep. Let a man strive as an athlete, when he has　　　55
studied the line that claims Kleonikos!
With them, great toil is never obscured, nor are the sums
spent to excite their ambition.
Pytheas too I would praise as a tamer of　　　victor's older brother
limbs. Clever of hand, his mind the same,　　　　　60
he set the course for Phylakidas' blows.
Take up his crown, bring him a cap made of
wool, and send out a soaring newly made song!

ISTHMIAN 6   The Engendering of Ajax

Again for Phylakidas of Aigina, son of Lampon, of the Psalychiad clan (line 64); the victory was taken in the boys' pankration, as in Isthmian 5, but evidently a year or so earlier, just before the battle of Salamis. The older brother, Pytheas, is again mentioned (line 57, cf. line 4), as is Euthymenes, a maternal uncle; here, however, it is Lampon, the father, who is given distinctive praise (lines 67–73), as patron, if not trainer, of young athletes.
Ca. 480 BC

1. Like men when the banquet bursts into bloom
we mix a second bowl, filled with songs from the Muses
meant for fine athletes fathered by Lampon.
    First, Zeus, they had from you a choice
Nemean crown and now this   won by Pytheas; see N. 5
youngest, Phylakidas, triumphs with   5
Isthmia's lord and the fifty
daughters of Nereus. Grant us a
third libation of honey-voiced song, to be
    poured out on Aigina
honoring Zeus as Olympian Savior!

Should a man toil, rejoice as he spends, then   10
touch upon god-given excellence, and should some power
engender the fame that he longs for, he may
    anchor his ship in the furthest
harbor of bliss, honored by
gods. That his temper be such,
as he encounters grizzled old age and   15
death—this Kleonikos' son asks, and   Lampon
I would beg Klotho the high-throned, with
    her sister Fates to
hear the entreaties made by my friend!

ep. My plainest rule as I walk this isle is to
rain praises down upon you, o   20
Aiakid drivers of golden cars! Your splendid
deeds have cut ten-thousand paths each a
    hundred feet wide, from the
source of the Nile to the lands beyond Boreas. No
city exists so wrong-tongued and brutish as
    not to have heard of the
glory of Peleus, hero made blessed and   25
    kin to the gods by his marriage, or

2. of Telemonian Ajax, or of that
father who readily followed Alkmena's   father=Telamon
son when he sailed off to Troy and the bronze clash of   son=Herakles
    battle, leading Tirynthian
men to punish Laomedon's
crimes. He took Pergamos, slaughtered the   30
Meropēs, and killed that
giant who loomed like a mountain   cf. N. 4.25–27
on Phlegra's plain—Alkyoneus the
    oxherd—nor were his hands
shy in their use of his deep-voiced bow, this

Herakles! Come to enlist his Aiakid   35
friend, he found a wedding and, as he stood
wrapped in his lion's skin, Telamon
    brought him a cup that bristled with
gold and asked that the first libation of
nectar be poured by Amphitryon's
son. He took it and, stretching his   40
masterful hands to the sky, spoke:
"If you have ever, o father Zeus, heard my
    prayers with a favoring heart,
hear me so now! Listen to this solemn plea:

ep. I beg that from Eriboia you bring, in
due time, a child—a bold son for this   45
man and a fated guest-friend for me!

Make his nature impervious,
  like to this pelt that
enwraps me, won from the beast that I killed in the first
contest at Nemea, and let his heart be the
  same!" In answer the
god sent an eagle, ruler of birds, and to   50
  him came a sweet inner joy   him=Herakles

3. as, like a prophet, he further proclaimed, "The
child you desire will be yours, Telamon!
Call him after this eagle-sign—Aias, the   eagle=*aietos*
  mighty, fearsome where
men work at war!" This said, he
sat, and the fair deeds that followed are   55
more than I can recount. I come, o
Muse, as keeper of revels for
Pytheas, Phylakidas, and Euthymenes,
  hence my speech will be
short—Argive, indeed in its brevity!

They took three pankratic crowns from the Isthmos,   60
others from well-shaded Nemea, these shining
boys and their uncle—what treasures of
  song they unearthed! With clear
dew from the Graces they sprinkle the
Psalychiads, as they dwell in this
city dear to the gods   65
restoring the house of Themistios.   maternal grandfather
Lampon spends zeal on his tasks, true to
  Hesiods's rule, which he   "Care makes work thrive" *WD* 412
honors and cites as he counsels his sons.

ep. He brings his city fine ornament, earns love with
kindness for strangers, seeks after   70
measure in judgment, then follows it—nor does his tongue
outrun his heart. Among athletes this
  man, you might say, is

Naxian stone, best for sharpening bronze. I
offer a draught dipped from Dirka's fair stream by   spring at Thebes
   gold-robed Mnemosynē's
deep bosomed daughters, close to the   the Graces
gates of the fortified city of Kadmos!   76

ISTHMIAN 7 A Brave Theban Warrior

For Strepsiades of Thebes, a youthful victor in the pankration. No father is named, and the ode gives most of its praise to a maternal uncle, also called Strepsiades, the son of Diodotos (line 30), who has died in battle (lines 23–35). Theban forces, with Peloponnesian allies, defeated the Athenians at Tanagra in 457 BC but were then routed by them in the following year at Oinophyta, where the uncle presumably was killed. 454 BC ?

1. Which ancient glory, o blessed Theba,
brings most joy to your heart? When you
raised up the long-haired god Dionysos to sit
throned with Demeter while cymbals clash?
Or when you welcomed the strongest of gods,   5
    come in a midnight snow-fall of

gold to the door of Amphitryon, seeking his
wife and bearing seed for the making of
Herakles? Is it Teiresias' prophetic counsels—
or Iolaos' skills as a driver? The
tireless Spartoi? Adrastos sent back from   10
    battle's loud cries to Argos, his

ep. city of horses, orphaned of ten-thousand
allies? Is it the Dorian outpost of
Lakedaimonians, fixed safely in place when
men sprung from you—the Aigeidai—
followed the Pythian voice to   legendary event of the 9th/8th c. BC
capture Amyklai? But old splendors   16
sleep and men are forgetful of deeds

2. that, never yoked to swift currents of words,
fail to arrive at the peak of song, so

173

dance to this hymn for Strepsiades!   20
He wears a pankratic Isthmian crown—
handsome to see, a marvel of strength, his
    courage no shame to his form!

Blazing with light from the dark-haired Muses,
he shares his crown with a like-named
uncle whose destiny Ares the bronze-armed   his mother's brother
compounded. Honor awaits a brave man.   26
Whoever rescues his land from a
    blood storm, turning it back on the

ep. enemy host, let him know this: his
life and his death both heighten the fame of
his fellow townsmen. You, o son of Diodotos,   you=the uncle of line 25
took as your model the fierce Meleager, with   31
Hektor and Amphiaraos, when you
breathed out your flowering youth in the
throng at the front, where the bravest of

3. warriors held fast, hopes stretched to the limit.   35
I knew unspeakable grief, but the Earthshaker now   Poseidon
sends me fair weather after the storm and
I mean to sing as I settle these crowns in my
hair. May the envy of heaven
    not be aroused, for I journey

quietly, tracking the joys of each day as I   40
move toward the end of my span. We do
all alike die, but our luck is not equal and
if a man gawks after far-distant
grandeurs he's ever too puny to reach to the
    bronze-floored home of the gods.

ep. So, when his master would enter the steadings of   45
heaven to hobnob with Zeus, winged Pegasos   cf. O. 13

threw off Bellerophon! Sweets that come counter to
justice carry the bitterest
taste in the end. O golden-haired
Loxias, grant us a flowering crown,   Apollo
gained in your Pythian contest!   51

ISTHMIAN 8   A Cosmic Monster Avoided

For Kleandros of Aigina, son of Telesarchos and cousin (or second
cousin) of Nikokles, another Isthmian victor who seems to be recently
dead (line 61). Kleandros is victor in the boys' pankration, as he had been
at Nemea (line 5), but he is leaving the class of the "beardless" (fifteen to
eighteen year olds), to compete from now on as an adult (lines 1, 70).

   This victory has come shortly after the battle at Plataia (479 BC),
where at least 1,500 Greeks lost their lives in the name of *eleutheria* (free-
dom, line 15, cf. 7) before the Persian invaders were defeated. To praise
one boy's victory in this context is difficult (lines 1–14), but it becomes
possible when both events are reduced to a common earthly scale by
comparison with an analogous cosmic contest.
Ca. 475 BC

1. Boys, for Kleandros
     and for his youth we must go to the
grand outer gate of his
sire, Telesarchos, to rouse up the
revel that offers a glorious ransom from toil—
     payment for victory taken at Isthmia
and for his Nemean dominance!   5
     Yes, I am asked, though I
sorrow, to call on the golden Muse.
Freed as we are from heaviest griefs, let's not
cherish our losses and cares, nor
orphan ourselves of crowns! Stubborn evils have
     come to an end so
let's meet together in sweet civic joy
after such pain! Hung as a menace over our   9
heads, the Tantalos stone has been   cf. O. 1.55–9
     shifted away by some god—that

2. task beyond bearing
    imposed upon Greece. But fear
left from the past yet
stops my strong impulse. Best keep an
eye on one's feet for a treacherous destiny
    hangs over all, twisting life's path. Yet
even such fear has its cure
    where men know freedom!
All should encourage good hope and
any man nurtured in seven-gate Thebes must
offer the Graces' best bloom to
Aigina! They were the two youngest daughters of
    Asopos, twins and
both of them pleasing to royal Zeus, who
settled the one close to the fair-flowing
waters of Dirka as queen of a
    town that loves chariots, while you he

3. carried to Oinopa's
    isle! He couched you and you gave him
Aiakos, godlike and
praised above all other men by his
thunder-voiced father. Among the immortals
    he served as judge and his sons, like theirs
lovers of war, surpassed all in the
service of bronze-clashing
battle while yet they were temperate
ever and prudent at heart. All this the
gathered immortals remembered when
Zeus and splendid Poseidon fell into contest
    over the couching of
Thetis, wanted by each as his beautiful
mate. Lust ruled over both but the
gods in their undying wisdom let
    neither one enter her bed,

4. once they had listened to
    heaven's decree as spoken by

fear's message?

15
eleutheria

as was Pindar

one=Thebe
20
you=Aigina

25

30

Themis the counselor.
She named this watery goddess as   goddess=Thetis
destined to bring forth a son mightier than his
    father—the bolt in his hand stronger than
lightning or tireless trident, should she be   35
    mated with Zeus or
one of his brothers. "Come," she said,
"this you must stop! Let her lie with a mortal
that she may watch as her son dies in
battle, though he be equal to Ares in
    strength, to a fire-bolt in
swiftness of foot! This is my counsel:
give her as heaven-sent bride-prize to Aiakid
Peleus, famed as the most pious man   40
    Iolkos' plain ever nourished.

5. My words must go, now,
    straight to the unchanging cavern of
Chiron, for Nereus'
daughter must not for a second time
bring us her dowry of discord. Instead, let her
    loosen her fair virgin halter on evenings at
midmonth, tamed by that hero!" She spoke,   45
    urging the children of
Kronos, and they in consent bowed their
immortal heads. Nor were her words without
fruit for, as we are told, the
two lords sanctioned this marriage for Thetis. For
    men as yet ignorant,
bardic tongues pictured the deeds of the   at the wedding?
youthful Achilles—he who bloodied the vine-rich
Mysian plain as drops of black gore   50
    rained down from Telephos. He   cf. O. 9.73; I. 5.41

6. bridged a return for the
    Atreids, set Helen free, and with his
lance cut out the sinews of
Trojans who tried for a time to

drag him away from his man-slaying work—Memnon,
  fierce in his pride, Hektor, and other great lords.
For them Achilles, favoring   55
  wind of the Aiakids,
opened a path to Persephonē's hall,
while he brought glory to Aigina and his own race.
Songs, when he died, did not desert him—
maidens of Helikon stood at his   Muses
  pyre and his tomb to
pour out their many-voiced threnody. It seemed
right to the gods that a brave man should be,
even in death, a theme for the   60
  hymns of these goddesses. This

7. rule yet holds true as the
  car of the Muses speeds out to
make a remembrance for
Nikokles and for his boxing.   a cousin
Praise one who captured the Doric garland at Isthmia and
  conquered all neighbors with fists that
none could escape! Nor is he   65
  shamed by the son of his
uncle and so, for Kleandros, one of his
age-mates must weave a rich pankratic crown made of
myrtle. Games held at Megara
gave him success and earlier,
  at Epidauros, the
boys made him welcome. He gives the
good man a reason to praise, for this is no
youth-time untried in fine deeds that he   70
leaves in the lair of a snake!   i.e., he has no cause for shame

From an ode for an unknown Aiginetan victor, boy or man; the event and
date are likewise unknown. This praise of the fundamentally Doric qual-
ity of Aigina can be compared with the similar praise of Hieron's Syr-
acuse in Pythian 1, lines 61–5.
Date unknown

Famed is the story of Aiakos, famed too is Aigina,
    known for her glorious ships! Divine
destiny sent, as her founders, the Dorian
host of Aigimios and Hyllos, and   first Dorian king / Herakles' son
her men still live by the law of those heroes,
never dishonoring heaven's decrees, never   5
failing in justice to strangers. In prowess like
dolphins at sea, they give wise care,
    both to the Muses and to the contests of athletes.

Selected Bibliography

For details of myths, see P. Grimal, *The Penguin Dictionary of Classical Mythology* (London, 1991).

Translations of Pindar

F. J. Nisetich. *Pindar's Victory Songs*. Baltimore: Johns Hopkins University Press, 1980.

W. H. Race. *Pindar*. Loeb Classics, 2 vols. Cambridge, Mass.: Harvard University Press, 1997.

A. Verity. *Pindar: The Complete Odes*. New York: Oxford University Press, 2007.

General Discussions

A. P. Burnett. *Pindar*. London: Bristol Classical Press, 2008.

C. J. Herington. *Poetry into Drama*. Berkeley and Los Angeles: University of California Press, 1985. Pp. 20–31, and Appendix IV, "The Performance of Choral Lyric," pp. 81–91.

R. W. Johnson. *The Idea of Lyric*. Berkeley and Los Angeles: University of California Press, 1982. Pp. 59–71.

F. J. Nisetich. Introduction to *Pindar's Victory Songs*. Baltimore: Johns Hopkins University Press, 1980. Pp. 1–77

G. B. Walsh. *The Varieties of Enchantment*. Chapel Hill: University of North Carolina Press, 1984. Pp. 37–61.

Concentrated Studies

A. P. Burnett. *Pindar's Songs for Young Athletes of Aigina*. New York: Oxford University Press, 2005.

D. S. Carne-Ross. *Pindar*. New Haven: Yale University Press, 1985.

S. Hornblower, C. Morgan. *Pindar's Poetry, Patrons and Festivals*. New York: Oxford University Press, 2007

L. Kurke. *The Traffic in Praise*. Ithaca: Cornell University Press, 1991.

H. Mackie. *Graceful Errors: Pindar and the Performance of Praise*. Ann Arbor: University of Michigan Press, 2003.

W. H. Race. *Pindar*. Boston: Twayne Publishers, 1986.

On Greek Athletics

E. Norman Gardiner. *Athletics of the Ancient World*. Chicago: University of Chicago Press, 1987.

S. G. Miller. *Ancient Greek Athletics*. New Haven: Yale University Press, 2004.

Register of Mythic Names
Mentioned in the Odes

Bold type marks the most significant passages.

Achilles: son of Peleus and Thetis; grandson of Aiakos; father of Neoptolemos. Educated by Chiron, best of the Achaeans at Troy, leader of the Myrmidons, he was celebrated as the slayer of Kyknos, Memnon, Hektor, and many others. Ajax and Odysseus defended his corpse when he fell by an arrow from Apollo; after funeral games his arms were granted to Odysseus. O. 2.79; O. 9.71; O. 10.19; **N. 3.43–63**; N. 6.49–53; N. 8.29–32; I. 5.39–42; I. 8.52–66.

Adrastos: Argive king and for a time ruler at Sikyon. After he returned to Argos, he became the ally of Polyneikes (q.v.) and led the Seven in the first expedition against Thebes. O. 6.13; P. 8.48–55; N. 8.51; N. 9.9–27; N. 10.12; I 7.10–11.

Aiakos: son of Zeus and the nymph, Aigina; father of Phokos, the seal-man, and also of Peleus and Telamon. As hero-founder of the Aiginetan polity, he was noted for justice and piety, and his prayers to Zeus rescued all Greece from famine, as memorialized at the island sanctuary of Zeus Panhellenios. After his death he served as a judge in the underworld. N. 5.53; **N. 7.82–4**; N. 8.13; **I. 5.33–8**; **I. 8.23–8**.

Aietēs: son of Helios; king of Kolchis; father of Medea; possessor of the Golden Fleece. (See Jason.) P. 4.10, 160, **211–39**.

Ajax: son of Telamon of Salamis; grandson of Aiakos. At Troy, he was second only to Achilles, whose fallen corpse he rescued; not granted the arms of Achilles, he leapt on his own sword. N. 2.14; N. 4.48; **N. 7.24–30**; **N. 8.23–33**; **I. 4.37–40**; I. 5.48; **I. 6.26–56**.

Akastos: king of Iolkos; husband of Hippolyta. As host of Peleus (q.v.), he plotted against his guest. **N. 4.54–60**; N. 5.26–8.

Alkmena: mother of twin sons, Iphikles (fathered by her husband, Amphitryon) and Herakles (fathered by Zeus). O. 7.27; P. 9.84–6; **N. 1.33–54**; N. 10.11; I. 1.12.

Amphiaraos: Argive prince and seer, son of king Oikleos. Opposed to Adrastos, then reconciled through Eriphyle (q.v.), he took part in the expedition of the Seven against Thebes; swallowed up in the earth there, his voice became that of an oracular shrine. **O. 6.12–21**; **P. 8.39–56**; N. 9.13, 24–7; I. 7.33.

Amphitryon: Argive husband of Alkmena (q.v.) and father of Iphikles, the mortal twin brother of Herakles. He fought as an ally of Herakles and after an accidental murder took refuge at Thebes, where he was later honored with games held at his tomb. P. 9.81–2; **N. l.51–8**; N. 4.19–21; N. 10.13–5; I. 1.55.

Apollo (Phoibos): son of Zeus and Leto; father of Asklepios (q.v.). A youthful lyre-player whose weapon was the bow, he was closely associated with the Muses. His major seat was at Delphi, where he spoke through the Pythian oracle and where athletic games and musical contests were held in his honor. O. 3.16; O. 6.35; **O. 8.31–47**; O. 14.11; P. 1.1; P. 2.16; **P. 3.8–58**; P. 4.5, 87, 176, 294; **P. 5.60– 81**; P. 7.8–9; P. 8.18; **P. 9.9–70**; P. 10.10, 34–6; N. 5.23–5, 44; N. 9.1; I. 2.18.

Ares: son of Zeus and Hera. God of war, his name often signifies violence or the act of making war. O. 9.76; O. 10.15; O. 13.23; P. 1.10; P. 2.2; P. 5.85; P. 10.14; P. 11.36; N. 10.84; I. 4.15; I. 5.48. I. 7.25; I. 8.41.

Artemis (Orthosia): twin sister of Apollo; virgin goddess of the hunt. **O. 3.26–30**; P. 2.7–9; P. 3.32–4; P. 4.90–2; N. 1.2–3; N. 3.50.

Asklepios: son of Apollo and Koronis. He was educated by Chiron as a healer of great power; when struck by the thunderbolt of Zeus for attempting to revive the dead, he was changed into a constellation and honored in parts of Greece as a god of healing. **P. 3.5–58**; N. 3.54–5.

Atreus: son of Pelops and Hippodameia; Mycenaean king; father of Agamemnon and Menelaos. O. 13.58; O. 9.70; P. 2.9; P. 11.31; I. 5.38; I. 8.56.

Augeas: king of Elis. He refused to pay Herakles (q.v.), who had cleaned his stables as his Sixth Labor, and so lost his city and his life to that hero. **O. 10.28–42.**

Bellerophon: son of Glaukos of Corinth; tamer of the winged horse, Pegasos. As an exile in service of the king of Lykia, he defeated the neighboring armies of the Solymoi and the Amazons and killed the monster Chimaera. **O. 13.60–92.**

Charitēs (Graces): Aglaia, Euphrosyna, Thalia; powers that lend enchantment to objects and actions; especially associated with Aphrodite and the Muses. O. 2.50; O. 4.10; **O. 9.27–8**; O. 14.4; P. 2.42; P. 6.2; P. 8.21; P. 12.26; N. 4.7; N. 5.54; N. 6.37; N. 9.54; N. 10.1, 38; I. 5.21; I. 6.63; I. 8.18.

Chiron: centaur, son of Kronos; wise teacher and healer. Many heroes were sent to his cave on Mount Pelion for education, including Jason, Asklepios, Achilles (q.v.), and it was he who arranged the marriage of Peleus and Thetis. **P. 3.1–7, 63–5**; P. 4.101–3, 115; **P. 9.26–66; N. 3.43–63**; N. 4.60–1; I. 8.45–6.

Danaë: daughter of Akrisios. While she was locked in a tower, Zeus came to her as a shower of gold to engender Perseus (q.v.). P. 10.45; P. 12.17; N. 10.11.

Danaos: king of Argos, originally from Egypt. He gave his fifty daughters, the Danaids, to the fifty sons of his brother, Aigyptos, with instructions to kill their husbands on the wedding night, and all but one obeyed (see Hypermestra); later the girls were given to bridegrooms who raced for them. **P. 9.111–6; N. 10.1–6.**

Demeter: daughter of Rhea and Kronos; goddess of grain-giving earth. By Zeus, she was the mother of Persephonē, with whom she was celebrated in the Eleusinian mysteries, with special cults in Sicily. O. 6.95; I. 1.57; I. 7.3–5.

Deukalion: son of Prometheus. In the Great Flood that ended the Bronze Age, he and his wife Pyrrha were the only survivors; directed by Zeus, they created a new race of Stone People made from pebbles. **O. 9.43–56.**

Dionysos (Bromios): son of Zeus and Semele; god of wine and Bacchic ecstasy. O. 2.26–7; O. 13.18–19; I. 7.3–5.

Eleithyia: goddess of childbirth. O. 6.42; P. 3.9; N. 7.1.

Endaïs: dryad, wife of Aiakos, mother of Peleus and Telamon. N. 5.12.

Enyalios: epithet of Ares, god of war. O. 13.106; N. 9.37; I. 6.54.

Epaphos: son of Zeus and Io, born in Egypt; father of Libya; ancestor of Danaos. P. 4.14; N. 10.5.

Erechtheus: authochthonous hero and early king of Attica; founder of the Panathenaic festival. P. 7.8; I. 2.19.

Eriphylē: sister of Adrastos (q.v.). Given to Amphiaraos to end the quarrel among the heirs to the Argive throne, she persuaded her husband to join the Seven in their attack on Thebes. N. 9.16.

Eunomia (Order): daughter of Themis; sister of Justice and Peace. O. 9.16; O. 13.6.

Eurystheus: ruler of Tiryns, Mycenae, and Midea. By Hera's trickery he gained power over Herakles (q.v.), from whom he demanded the Twelve Labors. O. 3.28–30; P. 9.80.

Ganymede: Trojan boy beloved of Zeus and taken to Olympus to be his immortal cupbearer. O. 1.44–5; O. 10.105.

Glaukos: grandson of Bellerophon (q.v.); Corinthian warrior at Troy. O. 13.60.

Gorgons: snake-haired female monsters—Euryalē, Stheno, and Medusa. To look at any one of them directly was to be turned to stone. (See Perseus.) P. 12.7–17.

Hebē (Youth): daughter of Zeus and Hera. The personification of ripe adolescence, she was given to Herakles as his bride when he came to Olympus. O. 6.58; P. 9.109; N, 1.71–2; N. 7.4; N. 10.18; I. 4.65.

Hektor: son of Priam, king of Troy; strongest of that city's warriors. Killer of Patroklos, he was in turn killed by Achilles. O. 2.81; N. 2.14; N. 9.39; I. 5.39; I. 7.32; I. 8.60.

Helen: daughter of Leda and Zeus, sister of Kastor, Pollux, and Klytemnestra. Married to Menelaos, the brother of Agamemnon, she was carried off by Paris and so became cause of the ten-year Greek siege of Troy. O. 3.1; O.13.59; P. 5.83; P. 11.33; I. 8.57.

Helios (the Sun): son of the Titan Hyperion; the father of Aietēs (q.v.) by the Oceanid, Perseis; lover of the nymph, Rhodos. **O. 7.14, 54–76**; P. 4.241; I. 5.1.

Hera: goddess of marriage fulfilled; sister-mate of Zeus; mother of Hebē and of Eleithyia; divine opponent of Herakles (q.v.). She was the principal deity at Argos, where games were dedicated to her. O. 6.88; P.2.27–8; P. 4.184; P. 8.79; **N. 1.35–45**; N.7.2, 95; N. 10.2, 23, 36; N. 11.2; I. 4.65–6.

Herakles: son of Zeus and Alkmena. Thought of as author of the Dorian race and its laws; he was known for Twelve Labors (forced on him by Hera's contrivance), among which were to kill a lion that terrorized Nemea, to capture a wandering hind dedicated to Artemis, and to clean the stables of Augeas, king of Elis. When

Augeas refused to pay, Herakles took Elis in retaliation and there established the Olympic Games. Cheated again by Laomedon, king of Troy, Herakles conquered that city, with Telamon and Iolaos, and killed the king. Taken from his funeral pyre to Olympus, Herakles was made immortal and was married to Hebē, the daughter of Hera. (See Laomedon.) **O. 3.10–34**; O. 6.67–70; **O. 9.29–35; O. 10.25–77**; P.1.62–5; **N.1.33–72; I. 6.35–56**.

Hermes: son of Zeus and Maia; messenger god, protector of heroes and travellers, with a special interest in athletic contests. **O. 6.77–81**; O. 8.81; P. 2.10; P. 4.178–9; P. 9.59–61; N. 10.51–4; I. 1.60–2.

Hestia (Hearth): virgin daughter of Kronos and Rhea; worshipped as the living center of household and city. **N. 11.1–10**.

Hippodameia: daughter of Oinomaos, ruler of Elis (Olympia). She was the bride of Pelops, who won her in contest. **O. 1.67–81**; O. 9.9–10.

Hippolyta: wife of Akastos, king of Iolkos. She was refused by Peleus (q.v.) when she attempted to seduce him. N. 4.54–8; **N. 5.25–36**.

Horai: Order, Justice, and Peace, daughters of Zeus and Themis; powers that protect the regular renewal of beauty and all that is valuable. O. 4.1; O. 13.17; P. 9.60; N. 8.1.

Hyllos: son of Herakles (by Deianeira or Omphalē). Adopted by the king of the Dorians, he was leader of the Heraklids after his father's death. One of the three Dorian tribes was named after him. P. 1.62.

Hyperboreans: fortunate race living beyond the North Wind, among whom Apollo spent part of each year. **O. 3.16–8, 31; P. 10.30–44**; I. 6.23.

Hypermestra: the one daughter of Danaos (q.v.) who spared her bridegroom. **N. 10.1–6**.

Hypsipylē: queen of the women of Lemnos, who had murdered their husbands and established an all female state. When the Argonauts came she welcomed them, arranged games, and herself became the mate of Jason. **O. 4.23–8**; P. 4.50–2, 251–6.

Iapetos: Titan father of Prometheus. O. 9.55.

Iolaos: nephew and favorite companion of Herakles. After Herakles' death, Iolaos attacked some of the hero's enemies, including Eurystheus, whom he killed; buried at Thebes near Amphitryon's tomb and commemorated in games held there. O. 9.99; **P. 9.78–83**; P. 11.59–61; N. 3.37; I. 1.16–7; I. 5.32; I. 7.9.

Iphigeneia: daughter of Agamemnon and Klytemnestra; sacrificed at Aulis in order to ensure favorable winds for the Atreid expedition against Troy. P. 11.22–3.

Iphikles: son of Amphitryon and Alkmena, mortal twin of Herakles, and his ally and companion. P. 9.84–8; I. 1.30.

Ixion: Thessalian king of Lapiths, who killed his father-in-law, was cleansed by Zeus and made immortal, then tried to rape Hera. **P. 2.21–48**.

Jason: son of Aeson, king of Iolkos; brought up by Chiron. He was challenged by his usurping uncle, Pelias, and led the Argonauts to Kolchis where, with the help of Medea (q.v.), he took the Golden Fleece. (See Phrixos.) **P. 4.67–256**; N. 3.53–4.

Kadmos: Phoenician founder of Thebes; killer of a dragon from whose teeth a population of Sown Men, or Spartoi, grew. Given Harmonia, daughter of Aphrodite and Ares, he fathered Ino and Semelē. O. 2.22–4; P. 3.88–93; P. 11.1–2.

Kastor: engendered by Tyndareus and born to Leda along with his immortal twin, Pollux (fathered by Zeus). As Dioscuroi or Tyndarids, the two were especially associated with the games at Olympia and with Sparta. O. 3.39; P. 1.66; P. 4.172; P. 5.9; P. 11.61–4; **N. 10.38, 55–90**; I. 1.31; I. 5.33.

Kinyras: king of Cyprus, beloved of Aphrodite and of Apollo. P. 2.15–7; N. 8.18.

Klotho: one of the three Fates or Moirai (the others are Lachesis, q.v., and Atropos). As daughters of Zeus and Themis, the Fates regulated individual destinies and even the actions of the gods. O. 1.26; I. 6.17.

Klytemnestra: daughter of Tyndareus and Leda; wife of Agamemnon, ruler of Argos; mother of Iphigeneia, Elektra, and Orestes. With her lover, Aigisthos, she murdered Agamemnon on his return from Troy, then after a time was herself killed by Orestes. **P. 11.17–37.**

Koronis: daughter of Phlegyas, king of the Lapiths; by Apollo, mother of Asklepios. **P. 3.5–44.**

Kronos: Titan husband of Rhea; father of Zeus and other Olympian gods. O. 1.10; O. 2.70; O. 4.8; O. 7.67; O. 8.17; O. 10.50; P. 2.39; P. 3.4, 94; N. 5.7; N. 11.25; I. 1.52.

Kyknos: son of Ares. A brigand who robbed travelers approaching Delphi, he offered his gains to his father. With Ares he resisted an attack by Herakles but was killed by that hero when caught alone. O. 2.82; O. 10.15; I. 5.39.

Lachesis: a Fate especially concerned with apportionment. (See Klotho.) O. 7.64.

Laomedon: one of the first kings of Troy; father of Priam. Having engaged Herakles to liberate his daughter, Hesionē, from Poseidon's monster, he refused him the agreed payment, so causing the siege of his city and his own death. N. 3.36; **I. 6.27–30.**

Leto: Titan; by Zeus the mother of Apollo and Artemis. She was especially associated with Delphi because in her defense Apollo there killed the giant, Python. O. 3.26; O. 8.31; N. 6.37.

Medea: daughter of Aietēs of Kolchis; granddaughter of Helios. Chosen by Aphrodite and given magical powers, she joined Jason and the Argonauts against her father. In Greece she contrived the death of Jason's enemy, Pelias; later in Corinth, when Jason chose to marry the local princess, she killed the two sons he had fathered. O. 13.53–4; P. 4.9–11, 212–23, 250.

Medusa: Gorgon (q.v.) beheaded by Perseus (q.v.). From her severed throat came the winged horse, Pegasos; her head became Athena's shield-device. **P. 10.46–8; P. 12.9–17**; N. 10.4.

Meleager: hero of the Calydonian boar hunt. He was held up as an example to Achilles (*Il.* 9. 524–99) as one who died in defense of his city. I. 7.32.

Melia: daughter of Okeanos; by Apollo mother of Ismenios and Teneros; worshipped at Thebes in the temple of Apollo Ismenios. P. 11.4–6.

Memnon: son of Eos (Dawn). An Ethiopian ally of the Trojans, he was strong enough to stand against Achilles; when Eos and Thetis intervened, Zeus gave victory to Achilles, immortality to Memnon. O. 2.83; P. 6.32; **N. 3.61–3; N. 6.50–3;** I. 5.40–1; I. 8.54.

Menelaos: son of Atreus, king of Mycenae; brother of Agamemnon; husband of Helen (q.v.), all of whose former suitors were bound by oath to defend his marriage. **N. 7.27–30.**

Mnemosynē (Memory): mother of the Muses. N. 7.15; I. 6.75.

Moliones: twin (or Siamese twin) sons of Poseidon. Allies of Augeas, they were killed when Herakles (q.v.) attacked Elis. O. 10.30–4.

Myrmidons: special force drawn from a war-loving Thessalian tribe (said to derive from Aigina) and commanded by Achilles. N. 3.13–7.

Nemesis: goddess of divine retribution. P. 10.44.

Neoptolemos: son of Achilles. Called to Troy at Achilles' death, he played a decisive role in the Greek victory (according to some sources, he was the killer of the aged Priam and the infant Astyanax). As king of the Molossians, in Epirus, he offered Trojan spoils at Delphi; after he was there killed by a stranger, he was honored with a hero's tomb in the Pythian sanctuary. N. 4.51; **N. 7.33–50, 103.**

Nereus: sea-god, father of fifty watery goddesses, the Nereids, one of whom was Thetis, mother of Achilles. (See Peleus.) O. 2.29; P. 3.92; P. 9.94; P. 11.2; N. 3.57; N. 4.65; N. 5.7, 36; I. 6.6; I. 8.47.

Nestor: king of Pylos; wisest of the Greeks at Troy; father of Antilochos. P. 3.112; **P. 6.28–43.**

Oinomaos: king at Pisa (Olympia); father of Hippodameia (q.v.). (See Pelops.) O. 1.70–81; O. 10.51.

Orestes: son of Agamemnon and Klytemnestra. Hidden at the time of his father's murder and brought up in Phokis, he returned to take vengeance on his mother and her lover when he came of age. **P. 11.15–37;** N. 11.34–5.

Orion: giant son of Poseidon. A great hunter, he was the beloved of many goddesses, including Dawn (Eos) and was finally changed into a constellation. N. 2.12.

Pallas: alternative name for Athena, emphasizing her virginity. O. 13.65–72; P. 12.7–27.

Patroklos: beloved battle companion of Achilles. **O. 9.70–9;** O. 10.19.

Peleus: son of Aiakos and Endaïs. Exiled from Aigina for killing Phokos, his seal-brother, he was cleansed by Akastos, king of Iolkos; when he rejected the advances of that king's wife, Hippolyta (q.v.), he was rewarded with the Nereid Thetis (a form-changer with whom he had to wrestle). After a magnificent wedding on Mount Pelion, he became the father of Achilles. O. 2.78; P. 3.87; P. 8.100; N. 3.32–6; **N. 4.54–68; N. 5.9–39;** I. 6.25; **I. 8.29–52.**

Pelias: son of Poseidon; usurping ruler of Iolkos; uncle of the rightful heir, Jason (q.v.), and instigator of the quest for the Golden Fleece. **P. 4.71–167, 250.**

Pelops: son of the Phrygian king, Tantalos (q.v.). He was said to have been butchered and served by his father as a feast for the gods, then recognized and reconstituted. A favorite of Poseidon's, he won Hippodameia (q.v.) in contest at Olympia and by her fathered Atreus, the father of Agamemnon. He was buried at Olympia. O. 1.36–96; O. 9.9–10; O. 10.24.

Persephonē: daughter of Zeus and Demeter. Carried off by Hades, she spent part of each year as queen of the Underworld and part on Olympus. With Demeter, she was at the center of the mysteries celebrated at Eleusis and was given special honors in Sicily. O. 6.95; O. 14.21; P. 12.2; N. 1.13–5; I. 8.60.

Perseus: son of Zeus and Danaë (q.v.). Locked in a chest with Danaë and thrown into the sea, he then washed up on Seriphos and was brought up by a fisherman. Challenged by the tyrant Polydektes to bring the head of Medusa, if he would defend his mother from rape, Perseus succeeded with Athena's help and used the trophy's magical power to destroy the tyrant and his friends. (See Gorgons, Medusa.) **P. 10.31–48; P. 12.9–18;** N. 10.4; I. 5.33.

Philoktetes: Thessalian warrior; possessor of the arrows of Herakles. He was put ashore on Lemnos on the way to Troy because of a festering wound, then sought out by Greek leaders, after the death of Achilles. At Troy, his wound miraculously healed, he made effective use of the fate-filled arrows. **P. 1.50–55.**

Philyra: by Kronos the mother of Chiron. P. 4.102–3; P. 6.22; N. 3.43.

Phokos: son of Aiakos and the Nereid Psammathē, part seal and born partly in the sea. Killed by his half-brothers, Peleus and Telamon, he had a hero-cult on Aigina. **N. 5.9–16.**

Phrixos: son of Athamas, a Boiotian king. He was offered as sacrifice by his stepmother but was rescued by a ram with golden fleece, who flew with him and his sister Hellē to Kolchis. The ram was sacrificed and its fleece placed under the protection of a dragon, to become the object of the expedition of the Argonauts. P. 4.159–63.

Pollux: son of Zeus and Leda; immortal twin of the mortal Kastor (q.v.). P. 11.61; **N. 10.50–90;** I. 5.33.

Polyneikes: son of Oidipous and Jokasta; father of Thersandros; brother of Eteokles, with whom he quarrelled for the Theban throne. Allied with Adrastos, he was one of the Seven who led the Argive expedition against Thebes, where he and his brother both died. O. 2.43.

Porphyrion: giant felled by Apollo's arrows during the giants' revolt against the gods. P. 8.12.

Poseidon: brother of Zeus; god of the sea, often called Earthshaker. The Isthmian Games were dedicated to him. **O.1.25–7, 40–45, 71–87;** O. 6.29, 103; O. 8.31, 48; O. 9.31; O. 13.5, 40; P.4.204; P. 6.50–1; N. 4.86; **N. 5.37–9;** I. 1.32, 52; I. 2.14; I. 4.60; **I. 8.29–52.**

Priam: king of Troy; traditionally the father of fifty sons, among whom were Hektor and Paris; also father of Kassandra. He was killed by Neoptolemos when Troy was taken. P. 1.54; P. 11.19; N. 7.35.

Proïtos: brother of Danaos, with whom he jointly ruled Argos. N. 10.41.

Protogeneia: granddaughter of a child (also named Protogeneia) of Deukalion and Pyrrha (q.v); daughter of Opous. Impregnated by Zeus, she became the wife of Lokris and through him made her son, the second Opous, the ruler of a city that mixed Stone People with Titans. **O. 9.41–66.**

Rhadamanthys: son of Zeus and Europa; inventor of Cretan law code; at death, appointed by Kronos as one of the judges in Hades (with Minos and Aiakos). O. 2.75; P. 2.73–5.

Rhea: daughter of Gaia and Ouranos; wife of Kronos; mother of Zeus, Poseidon, Hades, Hera, Demeter, and Hestia. O. 2.77; N. 11.1.

Sarpedon: son of Zeus; leader of a Lykian contingent allied with the Trojans; killed by Patroklos. P. 3.112.

Semelē: daughter of Kadmos; mother (by Zeus) of Dionysos. Struck by lightning as punishment for boasting of her liaison, she was eventually rescued from Hades by her son and established with the Olympians. **O. 2.25–7;** P. 11.1.

Sisyphos: wiliest of mortals; founder of Corinth. O. 13.52.

Tantalos: king of Phrygia; father of Pelops (q.v.). He is supposed to have offered his son to the gods as main course in a banquet. Himself made immortal by a divine gift of nectar and ambrosia, he tried to steal some of these substances and was punished by having an enormous stone hung over his head, while he suffered from hunger and thirst throughout eternity. **O. 1.36–64.**

Taÿgeta: one of the Pleiads; by Zeus mother of Lakedaimon. Pursued by Zeus, she was protected for a time by Artemis, who changed her into a doe; when finally taken she offered the goddess a doe with a gilded horn, which for a time caused damage to farmers and became the object of Herakles' Fourth Labor. **O. 3.25–30.**

Telamon; son of Aiakos and Endaïs; brother of Peleus; father of Ajax and Teukros. Exiled from Aigina, he settled on Salamis and later followed Herakles on the first expedition against Troy. P. 8.100; N. 3.37; **N. 4.25–30;** N. 8.23; **I. 6.26–56.**

Telephos: son of Herakles and Augē. As ruler (with Herakles) in Mysia when Greeks landed there by mistake, he drove them back to their ships, wounding Patroklos, but tripped on a vine and was himself wounded by the youthful Achilles. Later, in return for a magical healing, he directed the Atreid expedition toward Troy. **O. 9.70–3;** I. 5.41–2; I. 8.54–5.

Terpsichorē: Muse of the Dance. I.2.7.

Theia: daughter of Ouranos and Gaia; mother of Helios, Eos, and Selenē. The cosmic source of light, she made vision possible. I. 5.1.

Themis: goddess of Established Justice; daughter of Ouranos and Gaia. As second wife of Zeus (after Metis), she was mother of the Horai, the Fates, and Eunomia